The MS Warriors

A Love Story

Reversing Disability from Multiple Sclerosis Through Strength Training

David and Carol Phillipy

Forthcoming books by David A. Phillipy

Living in the Meantime traces the liturgical year starting with Advent, moving through Christmas, Epiphany and includes special days, including Lent/Ash Wednesday, the Baptism of Jesus, Trinity Sunday, the Transfiguration of Jesus, Christ the King, etc. The first chapter is "Living in the Meantime" and is based on the common lectionary. The question is how do we live in the meantime between the advent of Christ and the second coming of Christ in history?

Letters and Papers to and from Prison, is based on the model of the Pauline prison epistles, *Letters and Papers from Prison* based on the time Dietrich Bonhoeffer was in prison due to his participation to assassinate Hitler, and *Letter from a Birmingham Jail,* by Martin Luther King, Jr. The book has numerous photos of the places I have worked and the people I've met. This work is based on the letters I have received and written to inmates over the course of my prison chaplaincy career starting in 1968 in five different prisons, three different systems, and one mental institution to the present time, where I am a volunteer chaplain at Riverbend Maximum Security Prison.

Musings of a Sinner and Saint is my autobiography from childhood to the present time. It is inclusive of stories of me, my family, my education, the places I have worked and the very interesting people I have worked with. It is also filled with numerous photos.

The Walls Speak: A Story of Mass Incarceration in a Southern Prison, is a book about my years as a chaplain at Tennessee State Penitentiary, also known as "The Walls," from 1973 to 1983 and to its eventual closing in 1992. The work is a compilation of personal stories, internal memos, vignettes from documentary film material I shot, and legal documents and newspaper articles over the span of years. It is also filled with numerous pictures.

The MS Warriors

A Love Story

Reversing Disability from Multiple Sclerosis
Through Strength Training

David A. Phillipy

HenschelHAUS Publishing, Inc.
Milwaukee, Wisconsin

Disclaimer: While the activities presented in this book have worked
for the author and his wife, please consult your medical care
providers.

Published by
HenschelHAUS Publishing, Inc.
www.henschelHAUSbooks.com

ISBN: 978159598-500-2
E-ISBN: 978159598-503-3
LCCN: 2016951077

Printed in the United States of America.

*Dedicated to Carol
and all MS Warriors and their caregivers*

TABLE OF CONTENTS

FOREWORD

Rewiring of the brain is crucial to healing from MS. The book you are now holding will tell you how you can regain your strength, your memory, your vitality and your self-worth. MS is a lifelong disease without cure and one of the most common causes of disability in young adults in this country.

Having the privilege to know and to care for MS patients over the past thirty years, I marvel at the power of positive thinking, exercise, diet, spirituality, and love in healing MS.

In this book, David A. Phillipy lays out how MS had taken a physical and an emotional toll on Carol, his wife of three decades. Many of my patients could identify with Carol, with her disabilities and with her struggles to fight back against her MS. Carol's recovery, as chronicled in this book speaks, to the healing powers of determination, focus, love, and having a supportive relationship with your loved ones.

The author describes, step by step, how he and Carol did it and how you can, too! This book is not only inspiring, it is a testament to the fact that you can overcome some of the greatest challenges presented in MS. This book empowers you to look beyond what your physician can do for you; it challenges you to take control of your health and your body to conquer MS.

Read this book, get inspired, and be a MS warrior!

Bhupendra O. Khatri MD

Director, The Regional Multiple Sclerosis Center
& the Center for Neurological Disorders SC, Milwaukee, Wisconsin.
Author of the best-selling book, *Healing the Soul.*
Recipient of the 2016 Life Time Achievement award
from the National MS Society of America.

ACKNOWLEDGMENTS

With gratitude, we wish to thank the following for their contribution to this book: Wally and Belva Lane, Pam Reese, for their ideas and support. Thanks to Maryland Farms YMCA and the staff in Brentwood for their support. In particular, we wish to thank Holly Sanders, Operations Executive, and Corrie Marvin in the Wellness Center. We also thank Michael Sinclair-Whitely and Jeremy Pope for their help in the fitness center.

~ Carol and David Phillipy

INTRODUCTION

"Many waters cannot quench love, neither can floods drown it."
Song of Solomon 8: 7, RSV

My wife Carol has had Multiple Sclerosis, MS, since 1979, more than 35 years. She has relapsing MS, which used to be referred to as Relapsing Remitting MS, or RRMS. However, MS never remits. It always is active even in the absence of relapses. It never burns itself out, as some neurologists formerly believed.

Carol has not had any relapses since being on Betaseron, the first disease-modifying drug. Nor has she had any new lesions indicated on her Magnetic Resonance Imaging, MRI. However, MS runs silent and runs deep. It created ever-increasing disabilities in a variety of ways, especially over the past ten years.

Our experience suggests that the increasing disability was due to what some neurologists refer to as Secondary Progressive MS, or SPMS. This progression operates at a microscopic level and cannot be detected on with Magnetic Resonance Imaging (MRI).

A fairly recent study done by researchers at the University of British Columbia found that the interferon beta class of drugs does not prevent the onset of disability. The study found that these drugs, "had little or no effect on a patient's progress to disability ..."(1) It also found that these drugs did reduce the number of relapses and new brain lesions on the MRI. Further, "...there have

1

been few well-controlled studies demonstrating its effectiveness at preventing the onset of irreversible disability." (2) We will document later that increasing disability can not only be stopped, but reversed through an aggressive course of strength and flexibility training.

Having said that, Carol and I are warriors. This is a story of how she has fought the disease. This is also the story of how we together have fought the disease with me as her husband, caregiver and strength trainer. We are both warriors, as are many of our friends and caregivers. The ancient Samurai from Japan were known as *Bushido*, The Way of the Warrior. Carol and I are *Bushido*.

What causes MS?

It is not known what causes MS. However, there are some correlations. Many of the neurologists we hear speak indicate that the Epstein-Barr virus, which causes mononucleosis, sets the stage for MS. But not everyone who has the Epstein-Barr virus develops MS.

MS is an auto-immune disease in which the immune system mistakenly attacks the myelin, the fatty substance surrounding the nerves. When the nerves are exposed, they eventually die in the central nervous system, in the brain and in the spinal column. These lesions, or gaps, can then be seen on an MRI scan.

Another correlation is low vitamin D levels. According to Dr. Jerry Swanson, "The link between vitamin D and sunlight is strengthened by the association between sunlight and the risk of MS. The farther away from the equator a person lives, the greater the risk of MS. Sunlight is the most efficient source for vitamin D, suggesting that exposure to sunlight may offer protection from MS." (3) The neurologists we hear speak recommend 5,000 IUs a day as an optimal dose.

MS and Other Neurological Disorders

MS means "multiple scars." These may appear on a MRI of the central nervous system. MS can affect virtually any area of the body or mind and may vary considerably from one person to another. No two persons experience MS symptoms exactly alike. While this book is about reversing disability caused by MS, it is worth noting that progressive resistance training, PRT, has been useful in managing and reversing other neurological diseases, including post-polio syndrome, Parkinson's Disease and stroke.

In reference to PRT training with post-polio patients, James C. Agre, MD, PhD, explains,

> ... we conducted a 12-week study of muscle strengthening in seven post-polio subjects. Subjects exercised for four times a week for 12 weeks at home. Exercise intervals were interspersed with rest breaks. After the 12-week program, the average increase in strength was 36%. Also work capacity and endurance increased by 15% or more. (4)

Regarding Parkinson's disease, an article by Denise Mann states:

> Weight training may reduce the stiffness, slowness and tremors often seen in people with Parkinson's disease ... In the study, 48 people with Parkinson's disease participated in a weight-training program or another program aimed at improving flexibility, balance and strength. Participants exercised one hour twice a week for two years. They were aged 59, on average, and had had Parkinson's for about seven years. Everyone saw benefits after six months, but these benefits lasted two years in the weight-training group. (5)

Similar results were found for PRT with stroke patients. Authors Lee, Kilbreath, Singh, Zeman, and Davis state:

We have shown for the first time in a direct comparison study that high intensity PRT, but not cycling or sham exercise, can improve muscle strength, peak power, and muscle endurance in both affected and unaffected lower limbs after chronic stroke by a significant and clinically meaningful amount. Although strength gains plateaued earlier than anticipated, adherence to the intended high-intensity overload protocol was largely achieved.... (6)

"I was pushed hard so that I was falling, but the Lord helped me. The Lord is my strength and my song; he has become my salvation."
Psalms 118: 13-14 RSV

In Carol's and my experience, we have found an aggressive course of strength training (ST), in combination with resistance machines and free weights and flexibility exercises, has reversed Carol's disabilities on multiple matrices. (The abbreviations ST and PRT and Resistance Training, RT, may be used interchangeably, but for our purposes we will use the term ST.) Having said that, it is advisable to consult a physician before embarking on any exercise program.

This book is written in the hope that those who have MS may slow or possibly reverse the disabling effects of their disease. It is also written for spouses, family, caregivers, and medical professionals. I hope you may find this both inspirational and instructional.

~ David A. Phillipy

Introduction — Endnotes:

(1) Bakalar, Nicholas. "Multiple Sclerosis Drug Doesn't Prevent Onset of Disability, Study Finds," *New York Times*, July 18, 2012.

(2) Ibid.

(3) Swanson, Jerry W., MD, "Vitamin D and MS: Is there any connection," *Mayo Clinic*, February 4, 2016.

(4) Agre, James C., MD, PhD, "The Role of Activity," *Post-Polio Health*, Vol. 15, No. 2, Spring 1999.

(5) Mann, Denise, WebMD Health News, "Weight Training Improves Parkinson's Symptoms, Twice-Weekly Resistance Training Can Improve Tremors, Slowness and Rigidity," Parkinson's Disease Health Center, *WcbMD*, Feb. 16, 2012.

(6) Lee, MJ; Kilbreath, SL; Singh, SL; Zeman, B; Davis, GM, "Effect of progressive resistance training on multiple performance after chronic stroke," *Medical Science Sports Exercise*, 2010, January 42 (1), 23-34.

CHAPTER 1

AN UNWELCOME GUEST

~ MS SUCKS

C arol calls her MS "an unwelcome guest." I call that unwelcome guest a "sociopath." The sociopath shows no remorse or empathy. That's the way sociopaths are. They steal from body, mind and spirit. In their stealing, they create multiple stressors for those with MS, their spouses, family and caregivers.

This burglar has a long list of things which he steals. Areas affected include, but are not limited to:

♦ Diminished balance
♦ Loss of walking ability
♦ Excessive fatigue
♦ Numbness and tingling in limbs
♦ Loss of strength and dexterity in hands and fingers
♦ Changes in vision
♦ Dizziness and vertigo
♦ Cognitive problems, including concentration and memory
♦ Mood changes, including depression
♦ Muscle stiffness/spasticity

♦ Loss of bladder and bowel control

♦ Loss of sexual function, including diminished libido

This is the short list. Others with MS report diminished taste and smell, difficulty swallowing, speaking and hearing. Carol has had all of these, except depression, problems swallowing, speaking or hearing. MS sucks.

Prior to embarking on the strength training (ST) mission, the range of functions the sociopath stole included leg strength and balance, which increased the risk of falling while walking some distance. Energy levels have varied. Some of the side effects Carol experiences the next day after her Betaseron injection have been flu-like symptoms and diminished strength. I give her Betaseron shots every other night in hard-to-reach places, like her butt. I am officially her "shot meister."

A development beginning in August and September 2016 was a persistent increase in the loss of strength and balance. This reached a critical point on September 23, 2016, when Carol fell to the floor and could not get up on her own, without my assistance. (More on this in Chapter 2.) It took me two attempts to help get her to her feet. We had to get the walker from the car for greater safety and stayed home the rest of the day. Carol's strength then returned to baseline normal by mid-afternoon. The following day, we doubled her dose of Tylenol when she took her shot. On September 25, she was at baseline normal during the day and when we worked out.

Heat Sensitivity

Carol is also sensitive to heat, which is another MS symptom. Excessive heat short-circuits the nerves, resulting in excessive fatigue and more susceptibility to falling. In a study published in

2011, Swedish researchers found that more than seventy percent of all MS patients experience some degree of heat sensitivity. (1)

Any of these symptoms, in combination or by themselves, may be disabling. People may observe the balance and ambulatory problems that people with MS face, but those are only the tip of the iceberg. Beneath the tip of the MS iceberg are all of the other symptoms described above.

Sexual Dysfunction

As noted, the sociopath steals sexual pleasure. Sexual dysfunction is often a difficult topic to talk about between doctor and patients and between sexually intimate partners. Dr. Frederick Foley, PhD. notes that:

> Primary sexual dysfunction stems from MS-related changes in the brain and spinal cord that affect the sexual response or the ability to feel sexual pleasure. In both men and women, this can include a loss or decrease of sex drive, decreased or unpleasant genital sensations, and diminished capacity for orgasm. Men may experience difficulty achieving or maintaining an erection and a loss of ejaculatory force or frequency. Women may experience decreased vaginal lubrication, loss of vaginal muscle tone and/or diminished clitoral engorgement. (2)

Secondary sexual dysfunction does not directly involve nerve pathways but nonetheless impairs sexual pleasure. These symptoms may include bladder and bowel problems, spasticity, fatigue, muscle weakness, body or hand tremors and non-genital sensory changes, according to Dr. Foley. (3)

In addition, tertiary sexual dysfunction results from psychosocial and cultural issues that can interfere with one's sexual feelings and experience.

For sexual problems with men, the most frequent symptom is erectile dysfunction. Oral medications include Viagra®, (sildenafil citrate), Levitra®, (vardenafil HCI), and Cialis®, (tadalifil). Other more invasive forms include the implantation of a penile prosthesis but used only as a last resort.

Further, loss of libido is the most frequently reported symptom among women with MS. Currently, there are no medications that are effective for this symptom, though there have been case reports addressing this topic. In one study, sex therapy, in combination with symptom management and communication skills training, reported anecdotal success in women with MS. Behavioral re-training, which targets redevelopment of sexual pleasure in the absence of libido, has been reported.

The simplest solution for vaginal dryness and tightness is the use of water-soluble lubricants. Similar to the erectile response in men, vaginal lubrication is controlled by multiple pathways in the brain and spinal cord, some of which may be compromised in MS.

Of possible interest for those wish decrease in libido is *The Multiple Sclerosis Intimacy and Sexuality Questionnaire-19* (MSISQ-19). It was developed as a reliable and valid self-reporting questionnaire to assess the perceived influence of MS symptoms on the overall quality of intimate sexual relationships.

It is worth noting that from a research perspective, treatment of orgasmic loss in women with MS has been poorly studied.

At a personal level, Carol's libido had been absent several years. We tried water-soluble lubricants, but that was unsatisfactory. She was saddened at the prospect of never having an orgasm again.

The Sociopathic Unwelcome Guest

As of this writing, Carol is 69 years old. In 1978, there was no treatment for MS and no disease modifying drugs. When informing her of her diagnosis, Carol's neurologist told her there was nothing that could be done for her.

When we met December 1987, Carol told me she had MS but did not show any outward symptoms. When people marry, they do so with all the baggage each carries to the union. Traditional marriage vows carry the promise to "*love, honor and keep her for better or worse, for richer or poorer, in sickness and in health, and forsaking all others, be faithful only to her, as long as you both shall live.*" The parts "for better or worse" and "in sickness and in health" covers a lot of territory. We cannot predict the future. We cannot know how bad or good it may be. For us, it has been an amazing pilgrimage.

The first MS-disease-modifying drug to come on the market was Betaseron in the interferon class of drugs. It was approved for use in 1993. Carol could have been put on that drug at that time, but her neurologist never offered it to her. Further, he told her specifically, "Your MS has burned itself out."

MS never burns itself out. It never remits. In May 2003, Carol experienced a major exacerbation as we were preparing for a business trip to the Florida Gulf Coast. The sociopath attacked with fury. Before leaving home, Carol called her neurologist's office to get an emergency appointment. She was told the office no longer had her medical records and that she could not get an appointment until the paperwork was completed. We were told later by a nurse who worked with this neurologist that he no longer worked with MS patients.

We went to the business meeting in San Destin as planned, with Carol in a wheelchair, which her primary care physicians helped her obtain for the trip. At Fort Lauderdale, she peed on herself in the car as I was driving. She fell to the floor in a restaurant ladies room and I could not get her up. Navy personnel helped me get her to her feet and to a booth.

By Memorial Day, the relapse was so severe we went to the emergency room at Fort Walton Beach. We were fortunate in that the attending neurologist's wife had MS. He came from a Memorial Day cook-out to Carol's bedside in his Bermuda shorts. He reiterated the fact that MS never burns itself.

That MS relapse was particularly debilitating. Carol spent an extended period of time in a wheelchair. She started physical therapy, PT, upon our return home, and we found a new neurologist, who gave her information about disease-modifying drugs. She chose to go on Betaseron and has been on it ever since without a relapse.

Falls

As a result of that 2003 relapse, Carol's disabilities became increasingly more severe on a number of matrices. After getting out of the wheelchair, she walked with a cane for a period of time, but that was not adequate. She suffered frequent falls, so she began using a walker. In addition, we fitted the house with hand-rails to afford greater safety in the home.

The law of large numbers dictates that the more frequent the falls, the greater the likelihood of serious injuries. During her falls, Carol hit her head hard on the floor three times. On two of those occasions she was knocked unconscious. Once she fell forward and hit her forehead on the marble floor at the Frist Center for the

Visual Arts and was knocked out. She then taken to the emergency room at Vanderbilt Medical Center. Another time she fell backward and hit the back of her head on our hardwood floor with such force that her earrings flew off. Again she was knocked out and taken by ambulance to the ER. The Nashville Metro emergency responders have gotten to know us well.

Once, Carol fell and hit her right shoulder against the wall, dislocating the shoulder. She was taken to the ER and the dislocated shoulder was placed back in the socket. With arthroscopic surgery, three torn tendons were reattached, but one tendon remains detached. She went through a long period with her arm in a sling and extensive physical therapy, PT. The PT helped restore some of the range of motion, which remained limited. With normal range of motion, a person can reach over her head with her right hand and touch her left ear. Carol was only able to touch her right ear with her right hand, even after the PT.

Sometimes Carol's falls happen in the most awkward situations. Once she fell in the shower and could not get up. We turned off the water and she had to crawl out on her hands and knees. On another occasion, she fell while rising from the toilet and had difficulty getting out of the confined bathroom space. She had to crawl out of the toilet area to get up. Falling in cramped spaces presents a serious challenge.

Carol's other falls resulted in two broken wrists and a fractured shoulder, all of which required visits to the ER. In addition due to lack of strength and dexterity in her hands and fingers, she severely cut her finger while preparing food in the kitchen. This required another ER visit. Also, she fell in her office, hitting her head on the computer keyboard and suffering a gash on her eyebrow. Another ER visit requiring stitches. On still another occasion, she fell and hit her head on the cabinet under the kitchen sink, totaling the door of the cabinet. No injury to her noggin, though.

On one occasion, with only her cane, she fell when taking an escalator down at the Regal theatre in Green Hills. She and I had great difficulty getting her up as the escalator continued to move relentlessly downward.

Affectionately, I call Carol a one-woman wrecking ball. She is like a train that has jumped the track, or a car wreck. She sometimes destroys our belongings and property, and more worrisome, severely hurts herself. This is true, even though these events have reduced in number.

There are far-reaching effects of a fall. We have friends with MS who have broken bones as a result of falls. Fall injuries requiring medical attention rise almost linearly from age eighteen, peaking at 115 per 1,000 adults age 75 or older.

Fall statistics among older people are indeed daunting. Dr. Laurence Z. Rubenstein, the chairman of geriatrics of the University of Oklahoma College of Medicine reports that those 65 or older constitute about 13 percent of the population, but account for three-fourths of all deaths caused by falls. About 40 percent of this group fall at least once a year; one in 40 of them end up in a hospital, after which only half are still alive a year later. (4)

Aging, coupled with MS, represents a potentially dangerous combination. Having said that, research shows that ST can slow the loss of muscle mass in older adults. "Research that examined isometric force production characteristics during the aging process reports that the earliest declines in strength occur around age 40, in the forearm extensors and the muscles of the lower leg (dorsiflexors and plantar flexors). While the greatest overall loss of strength occurs in the two lower leg muscles (dorsiflexors and plantar flexors)." (5)

There have been numerous visits to our home by the Metro Nashville Fire Department emergency squad. On three occasions during the night, Carol fell to the bedroom floor transferring from the bed to the bathroom. She was so weak she was unable to get to her feet and I was totally helpless to assist her. Her legs were like lead. Getting to her feet was more difficult due to the fact that her right arm was in a sling because of her shoulder dislocation as noted above. It took three firemen to help her to her feet, get her to the toilet, and help her back to bed safely.

Another time when she attempted to transition from the bed to the toilet and fell on the floor, I couldn't get her up. We used a bedpan on the floor so she could void. Those times she remained on the floor with a pillow and blanket to cover her until the morning, when I could help her to her feet.

Once Carol fell in the parking lot of a restaurant. It was a very hot day. The asphalt pavement was scalding and no one heard her cry out for help, hence no one came to her assistance. Eventually, a driver saw her and got help from the restaurant employees, who brought her into the safety and air-conditioned security of the establishment. We know of one woman who fell in her backyard while hanging clothes on her outdoor clothes line on a very hot day and could not get to her feet or get help. She died of heat exhaustion.

Whenever Carol fell in our home, our dog Zach, a small Maltese, would begin barking. We always praised him for doing so. If I was home, I knew something was wrong and would go to her aid. Zach's barking does not always mean Carol needs help; sometimes, he just wants to play.

In all of the above situations, I felt utterly helpless trying to get Carol to her feet. I could not lift her up as I was not that strong even though I work out regularly. Whenever I hear her fall, I always fear the worst. The stress I experienced in those situations was enormous. "Things that go bump in the night" or day caused great alarm. I felt helpless.

The Financial Burdens from Disability

As a result of the shoulder injury and her arm being in a sling, Carol was unable to perform the duties of a financial advisor. Furthermore, she was unable to use the computer or drive a car. Using the phone was also more difficult. She was disabled to the point of being unable to work, and we incurred heavy debt as a result. A mistake we made was not applying for Social Security Disability Insurance, SSDI, as soon as she was deemed disabled. At a later date, she was not eligible.

In response to the oppressive debt, we sharply reduced our spending. In addition, at age 62, I qualified for and obtained a reverse mortgage, which eliminated our mortgage payment. We make ends meets with both our incomes from Social Security. I also have a state pension and a small pension from the Board of Pensions of the Presbyterian Church USA, in addition to some modest investment income. We are out of debt, are able to save, and have an emergency fund.

Weighty Problems

The difficulty getting Carol to her feet was worsened due to obesity. When we met December 1987, she weighed 160 pounds. In December 1989, when we married, she weighed 145 pounds. Over the years, she gained and lost weight, but in time, put on a lot of weight. At one point, she weighed 200 pounds. When she fell, I simply could not get her to her feet.

I tried not to nag Carol on her excessive weight. My approach from time to time was to ask her to lose the weight for me so it might be easier for me to help her to her feet when she fell. Health benefits were mentioned as well when we talked about it. However, motivation comes from within. The motivation to lose weight had to be on her terms, not mine.

Comorbidities

Of course, excessive weight compounds MS-related disabilities. It exacerbates fatigue, balance, endurance, walking speed and walking distance. Excessive weight places an extra burden on legs already weakened by MS.

Imagine placing fifty pounds on your back all at once and carrying that around for a day. Anyone, and especially someone with MS, would notice immediately the increased difficulties. When we gain weight over time, we do not notice the effects since they are so gradual. It is like putting a frog in water at room temperature and slowly raising the water to boiling. The frog will not attempt to get out but will still be cooked to death.

There are many comorbidities associated with obesity. In "A New Paradigm for MS Care—Optimizing Health Through the Integration of Lifestyle, Alternative and Conventional Medicine," presented by Allen Bowling, MD, PhD at the annual meeting of the Consortium of MS Centers, Dr. Bowling reviews a few of the comorbidities and their effect on overall health. (6)

For mental health, Bowling identifies depression and anxiety, bipolar disorder, seizure disorders, and alcohol abuse. Physical comorbidities in people with MS often include high cholesterol, high blood pressure, arthritis, irritable bowel syndrome, and chronic lung disease according to his presentation.

All of the obesity and related comorbidities include, in addition to high cholesterol and high blood pressure, heart disease, obstructive sleep apnea and stroke.

Obesity presents an ever-increasing risk as people with MS are placed in wheelchairs and activity levels decrease, thus leading to a vicious cycle of more weight. "There is an inverse relationship between activity levels in disabled subjects," says Y. Dionyssiotis, in an article on body composition in multiple sclerosis, "depending on the degree of mobility impairment, which leads to reduced physical activity. (7) This is the case in MS: the reduced activity needs to be accompanied by a reduction in energy intake otherwise body fat will increase."

Additional evidence suggests that childhood obesity in adolescents increases the risk of developing MS by age twenty. According to Sue Hughes, in her 2014 *Medscape* article, "Obesity Linked to Increased Risk for MS":

> Obesity in adolescence or early adulthood is associated with increased risk for multiple sclerosis, (MS) a new study suggests. ... For the current study, Body Mass Index (BMI) was calculated for 210 patients with MS and 210 controls of the same age and sex who did not have MS at ages 15 and 20 years and at the time of the study. Results showed that people who are obese (BMI ≥ 30 kg/m^2) at age 20 are twice as likely to develop MS as people who are not obese.... (8)

Another study corroborated the link between childhood obesity in girls and the development of MS later. "A new study of 75 kids with MS finds that extremely obese girls may be as much as four times more likely to be diagnosed with the condition as non-overweight girls," states Jeffrey Kopman in *Everyday Health.* (9)

Other Comorbidities and MS

Urinary tract infections, UTI, are a frequent comorbidity of MS. UTI has been a frequent problem for Carol. We have found several things helpful for treating her UIT. These include a prescribed vaginal estrogen cream three times a week, 100 mg Trospium chloride daily, 25 mg cranberry concentrate pills twice a day and 1,000 mg Vitamin C twice a day. The Trospium chloride and estrogen cream were essential in stopping recurrences.

There is also a greater risk for other autoimmune conditions. According to Ruth Ann Marrie, MD, "... more than 7 percent of people with MS have psoriasis, over 6 percent have thyroid disease and nearly 3 percent have RA (Rheumatoid Arthritis)." (10)

Factors other than MS may play a role, such as aging, lifestyle and smoking.

Additional comorbidity symptoms associated with MS include Ehlers-Danlos Syndrome (EDS) Hypermobility Type and Joint Hypermobility Syndrome. A study discussed by Claire Smith on WebStat.com, stated:

> ... in the Multiple Sclerosis population, there exists over 10 percent more Ehlers-Danlos patients than in the normal population. This percentage is even higher if statistics relating to the prevalence of EDS in the population is based on US figures rather than the UK's figures. Studies are indicating a form of external communicating hydrocephalus in the Ehlers-Danlos population, and the hypothesis is that the same type of hydrocephalus may occur in the Multiple Sclerosis population. (11)

Another comorbidity is the relationship between MS and Pseudo-bulbar Affect Syndrome (PAS), which is characterized by inappropriate laughter or crying, laughter without mirth and crying without sadness. This also known as Pathological Laughter or Crying, PLC. According to Dr. Anthony Feinstein, "approximately 10 percent of MS patients are affected with varying degrees of severity." (12)

This broad body of research supports our prescription of the need for strength training (ST) for those who have MS to ward off increasing disability or possibly reverse disabilities. Controlling weight and reversing obesity also needs to be done with ST, coupled with calorie reduction.

Depression, Suicide, and Self-Harm

Coupled with depression, both attempted and completed suicides rise dramatically in those with MS. A peer-reviewed study of Swedish and British discussed by Kristina Fiore, staff writer for *MedPage*, in Sweden, states:

> ... patients with MS are at a higher risk of suicide, as well as suicide attempts and other types of self-harm compared with the general population. ... MS patients are at twice the risk of completing suicide than the general population. They also attempted suicide at more than twice the rate compared with healthy controls...... A separate British registry found that the risk of any type of self-harm was higher by almost 60 percent in MS patients compared with the general population. (13)

Other forms of self-harm are mentioned in Ms. Fiore's article, but I could not find any information on non-suicidal self-injury (NSSI), which is self-harm without suicidal intent and correlated with MS patients. However, NSSI is recognized as a distinct diagnosis in the *Diagnostic and Statistical Manual of Mental Disorders* (DSM-IV-TR, 4th Edition). As a prison chaplain and chaplain at a state mental institution, I saw many cases of NSSI. While I could not find any empirical studies of NSSI as related to MS, I suspect there may be a correlation and feel that additional study is necessary.

Loss of Muscle Tone and Spasticity

Prior to embarking on our course of strength training, the range of functions the MS sociopath stole from Carol included balance, leg strength and the ability to walk any significant distance before the risk of falling. Her energy levels have varied. Some of the side effects of the Betaseron injection on the day following the shot include flu-like symptoms, muscle weakness and fatigue. Dexterity in her fingers was frequently compromised as she often dropped things. Muscle stiffness/spasticity have been common and cramping in the legs and feet.

Carol also experienced foot drop, which is the inability to lift the front part of the foot due to weakness or paralysis, causing the toes to drag along the ground when walking. Some people with foot drop may lift their knees higher than normal or may swing their legs in a wide arc. (14)

Spasticity and leg cramps were also a problem for Carol. She has compared it to her legs being as stiff as a board. Spasticity has been likened by some to walking in mud. We have learned that there are two forms of severe MS-related spasticity from the MS Society. First, in *flexor* spasticity, mostly involving the hamstrings, (the muscles on the back of the upper leg and hip flexors) muscles on the top of the upper thigh. The knees are bent and difficult to straighten. Second, in *extensor* spasticity, muscles involving the quadriceps and adductors (muscles on the front and inside of the upper leg), the hips and knees remain straight with the legs very close together or crossed over at the ankles. (15)

In addition to medication, treatment of spasticity includes physical therapy, occupational therapy and surgical measures for those rare cases that defy all other treatment.

According to Sue Kushner, MS, PT and Kathi Brandfass, MS PT, in *Information for Health Professionals* provided by the MS Society:

> General conditioning can also help to strengthen weak and deconditioned muscle groups and increase endurance and cardiovascular conditioning. Strengthening can be achieved in a variety of ways, using free weights, machines, stretch bands, Swiss balls or aquatic exercise. Strength training can also assist in the timing of movements depending on the strength or weakness of the agonist/antagonist muscles. (16)

Carol used to have extensor spasticity affecting the quadriceps down to her ankles. Since we began strength and flexibility training, she almost never has this type of spasticity any longer. Cramping occurred primarily in her feet. More about this later.

The MS "Hug"

Somewhat similar to spasticity is another symptom Carol experienced—the MS "hug," in the early stages of her disease. She describes it as if someone had their arms around her waist. Over the last few years, the "hugs" have decreased in frequency. Strength training had no impact on the "hug," and she longer experiences it.

The "hug" is an abnormal sensation caused by a lesion on the spinal cord. This neuropathic pain is called a "paresthesia" and is the result of the tiny muscles between the ribs going into spasm.

The "hug" itself is different for everyone, and it can also differ within one person every day, week, or month. It may not only occur in the stomach region, but also low in the waist or high in the chest.

It can give a person trouble on one side of the body or both sides. Stress and fatigue may trigger it. The hug can last for minutes or years, and range from anywhere between a slight tickle to a stabbing pain, according to Cathy Chester via MultipleSclerosis.net. (17)

Comorbidities and MS

The issue of excessive weight raises concern about the many comorbidities associated with MS. These conditions may be inclusive of, but go beyond, the usual list of MS symptoms and require treatment in their own right.

Mental comorbidities include depression and cognitive impairment. According to researchers P.I. Jongen, A.T. Ter Horst, and A.M. Brand, "Cognitive impairment occurs in 45-65% of multiple sclerosis patients typically involving complex attention, information processing speed, (episodic) memory, and executive functions." (18)

Further, the National MS Society, in its "Cognitive Changes" information, states: "Cognitive problems are only weakly related to other disease characteristics—meaning a person with almost no physical impairments can have significant cognitive impairment, while a person who is quite disabled physically can be unaffected cognitively." (19)

When you begin losing your cognitive functions, this is similar to the computer HAL in *2001: A Space Odyssey.* "I'm afraid, Dave. Dave, my mind is going. I can feel it. I can feel it. My mind is going. There is no question about it. I can feel it. I can feel it."

Indeed, it is frightening for both the person with MS and caregiver alike. Carol's long-term memory is excellent. Yet her short-term memory has resulted in getting lost when driving to a destination she is not familiar with. She always carries her cell phone in her car when she drives in case of an emergency. On more than one occasion, she has called me to tell me she was lost. I would try to help her find her way by her looking for landmarks.

The Impacts of Smoking

A further contribution to cognitive decline is smoking tobacco. According to new research, smoking can hinder brain function and not just among the elderly, as previously thought. A new study published in the journal *Stroke* linked the well-studied, proven cardiovascular risks to cognitive decline even among younger adults.

Researchers found that smoking as little as even one cigarette a day can decrease cognitive ability and smoking more than 15 cigarettes daily inhibits critical thinking and memory by as much as two percent. The reason for this drop in brain power is directly linked to the harm that is done to the heart.

When there's damage to the heart vessels, there's also likely damage to the brain vessels," says study author, Dr. Hanneke Joosten of the University Medical Center in the Netherlands. "This is especially important for young adults to realize because the burdens of unhealthy lifestyle choices often go unnoticed." (20)

Couples who smoke compound the problem. Second-hand smoke exacerbates the problem for the non-smoking spouse with MS.

Poop Happens

Loss of bladder and bowel control was very problematic for Carol. She frequently peed on herself, sometimes in public situations. She experienced bowel problems with constipation on one hand and loose bowels on the other. Carol had frequent episodes of fecal incontinence, which I call "projectile pooping."

Of course, as her caregiver, I had to clean up the mess. All these episodes caused me considerable stress. I came to refer to myself as the "poop meister."

One of the neurologists who speaks regularly at MS dinners sponsored by pharmaceutical companies said that some people who experience loss of bladder and bowel become virtually homebound due to the fear of having an accident in public.

Carol and I could not go to a movie without the justifiable fear that she would pee on herself before she could get from the theatre to the ladies room.

In addition, as a result of the limited range of motion in her right arm, Carol has difficulty wiping herself after a bowel movement. In my role as "poop meister," I help her wipe herself after a bowel movement with a wet washcloth. I joke about this and tell her she is going to have to double my pay. In addition, her disabilities were increasing on multiple scales.

The Expanded Disability Status Scale

On the Expanded Disability Status Scale (EDSS) developed by late neurologist John F. Kurtzke, MD, the following systems are compromised in people with MS: pyramidal (ability to walk), cerebellar, (coordination), brainstem, sensory (touch), bowel and bladder, visual and cerebral.

The assessment rates the ability to walk on a 10-point scale. The limitation is that it measures only the ability to walk, but not coordination, bowel and bladder, visual, cognition, fatigue, sexuality and other forms of MS disabilities. These need to be measured clinically and by self-monitoring. On this scale, being normal is 0.0. Being quadriplegic in bed, but able to eat and talk is 9:0. Death due to MS is 10. (21)

Kurtzke Expanded Disability Status Scale (EDSS)

❏ 0.0 - Normal neurological exam (all grade 0 in all Functional System (FS) scores*).

❏ 1.0 - No disability, minimal signs in one FS* (i.e., grade 1).

❏ 1.5 - No disability, minimal signs in more than one FS* (more than 1 FS grade 1).

❏ 2.0 - Minimal disability in one FS (one FS grade 2, others 0 or 1).

❏ 2.5 - Minimal disability in two FS (two FS grade 2, others 0 or 1).

❏ 3.0 - Moderate disability in one FS (one FS grade 3, others 0 or 1) or mild disability in three or four FS (three or four FS grade 2, others 0 or 1) though fully ambulatory.

❏ 3.5 - Fully ambulatory but with moderate disability in one FS (one grade 3) and one or two FS grade 2; or two FS grade 3 (others 0 or 1) or five grade 2 (others 0 or 1).

❏ 4.0 - Fully ambulatory without aid, self-sufficient, up and about some 12 hours a day despite relatively severe disability consisting of one FS grade 4 (others 0 or 1), or combination of lesser grades exceeding limits of previous steps; able to walk without aid or rest some 500 meters.

❏ 4.5 - Fully ambulatory without aid, up and about much of the day, able to work a full day, may otherwise have some limitation of full activity or require minimal assistance; characterized by relatively severe disability usually consisting of one FS grade 4 (others or 1) or combinations of lesser grades exceeding limits of previous steps; able to walk without aid or rest some 300 meters.

❏ 5.0 - Ambulatory without aid or rest for about 200 meters; disability severe enough to impair full daily activities (e.g., to work a full day without special provisions); (Usual FS equivalents are one grade 5 alone, others 0 or 1; or combinations of lesser grades usually exceeding specifications for step 4.0).

❏ 5.5 - Ambulatory without aid for about 100 meters; disability severe enough to preclude full daily activities; (Usual FS equivalents are one grade 5 alone, others 0 or 1; or combination of lesser grades usually exceeding those for step 4.0).

❏ 6.0 - Intermittent or unilateral constant assistance (cane, crutch, brace) required to walk about 100 meters with or without resting; (Usual FS equivalents are combinations with more than two FS grade 3+).

❑ 6.5 - Constant bilateral assistance (canes, crutches, braces) required to walk about 20 meters without resting; (Usual FS equivalents are combinations with more than two FS grade 3+).

❑ 7.0 - Unable to walk beyond approximately 5 meters even with aid, essentially restricted to wheelchair; wheels self in standard wheelchair and transfers alone; up and about in wheelchair some 12 hours a day; (Usual FS equivalents are combinations with more than one FS grade 4+; very rarely pyramidal grade 5 alone).

❑ 7.5 - Unable to take more than a few steps; restricted to wheelchair; may need aid in transfer; wheels self but cannot carry on in standard wheelchair a full day; May require motorized wheelchair; (Usual FS equivalents are combinations with more than one FS grade 4+).

❑ 8.0 - Essentially restricted to bed or chair or perambulated in wheelchair, but may be out of bed itself much of the day; retains many self-care functions; generally has effective use of arms; (Usual FS equivalents are combinations, generally grade 4+ in several systems).

❑ 8.5 - Essentially restricted to bed much of day; has some effective use of arm(s); retains some self-care functions; (Usual FS equivalents are combinations, generally 4+ in several systems).

❑ 9.0 - Helpless bed patient; can communicate and eat; (Usual FS equivalents are combinations, mostly grade 4+).

❑ 9.5 - Totally helpless bed patient; unable to communicate effectively or eat/swallow; (Usual FS equivalents are combinations, almost all grade 4+).

❑ 10.0 - Death due to MS.

---

*Excludes cerebral function grade 1.

Note 1: EDSS steps 1.0 to 4.5 refer to patients who are fully ambulatory and the precise step number is defined by the Functional System score(s). EDSS steps 5.0 to 9.5 are defined by the impairment to ambulation and usual equivalents in Functional Systems scores are provided.

Note 2: EDSS should not change by 1.0 step unless there is a change in the same direction of at least one step in at least one FS.

Sources: Kurtzke JF. Rating neurologic impairment in multiple sclerosis: an expanded disability status scale (EDSS). Neurology. 1983 Nov;33(11):1444-52.

Haber A, LaRocca NG. eds. Minimal Record of Disability for multiple sclerosis. New York: National Multiple Sclerosis Society; 1985.

Before we began Carol's strength training regimen, she would have rated 6.0, needing constant bilateral support (cane, crutch, walker or braces), required to walk 20 meters without resting. As of November 9, 2015, using a walker, she was able to walk 1,000 meters without resting. This measurement was taken at the office of Dr. Samuel Hunter, MD, PhD, of the Advanced Neurosciences Institute, to see if she would qualify for a clinical trial. This was much better than the previous 6.0. Today, she can walk 1,000 meters (1 kilometer, or .6 miles) and much more without resting. She has also improved on cerebellar, sensory, bowel and bladder, and multiple other ways through training.

Issues of Aging—Loss of Muscle Mass, Menopause, Osteoporosis

Loss of muscle mass in the aging process is a major contributor to disability in both the pyramidal and cerebellar systems, causing what is known as "sarcopenia."

According to *American Fitness*, it is further noted that, "inactive aging is associated with significant amounts of muscle loss on a year-by-year basis. Adults who do not perform some type of strength training sacrifice more than five pounds of muscle tissue every decade and older adults lose even more than that."(22)

Research has found that "on average, a woman over 25 years old who *doesn't* do strength training loses about one-half pound of muscle each year, or roughly 5 pounds in a decade." (23)

Loss of muscle mass makes a person feel weaker and look flabbier, and results in about a 3% decrease in resting metabolic rate (RMR). Over time, this slowing metabolism can lead to an increase in body fat.

What this means over the long-term is that from ages 25 to 65, people who do not do strength training will lose 20 pounds of muscle mass. While losing muscle mass, most Americans will gain fat. These factors, coupled with MS, make a walking disability more likely.

Carol has not lost muscle mass, as evidenced by recent new highwater marks on the weight she can push. I have lost muscle strength since January 2014 in my arms and abdominal core, and can no longer push the weight I used to. This can't be attributed to anything other than just getting older. I am 76 as of this writing. Just think how much worse this would be if we weren't doing strength training. Over the past two or so years, we have reduced the number of hours we do strength training from 8.5 hours per week to 4.5 a week.

Menopause

Another factor contributing to MS progression and disability in women is menopause. Research has demonstrated that link. Dr. Riley Bove, recipient of a Clinician Scientist Development Award, co-sponsored by the (MS) Society and the American Brain Foundation, gathered information on MS during menopause from 391 women enrolled in a large-scale, long-term study at Brigham and Women's Hospital in Boston.

The results showed that disease progression changed at or around menopause toward a more rapid accumulation of disability. Further research will determine whether such hormonal shifts are responsible for additional disability, "which may lead to a solution for women with MS going through menopause." (24)

Walking Can Help

The benefits of walking and moderate weight training have been shown to significantly reduce the chance that a frail older person will become physically disabled, according to one of the largest and longest-running studies of its kind to date. Dr. Marco Pahor, director of the Institute of Aging at the University of Florida in Gainsville and the lead author of the study, states:

> For the first time, we have directly shown that exercise can lessen or prevent the development of physical disability in a population of extremely vulnerable people. (25)

In the study, the exercise group received information about aging, but also started a program of walking and lower-body weight training with ankle weights, going to the exercise center twice a week for supervised group walks on a track, with the walks growing progressively longer. Study participants were also asked to complete three or four more exercise programs at home, aiming for a total of 150 minutes of walking and about three 10-minute sessions of weight-training exercises each week. (26)

Brain Shrinkage

Brain shrinkage, particularly in the hippocampus, the memory center of the brain, is also associated with aging. The *Los Angeles Times* reported a study, in which 120 older people who didn't exercise regularly, were recruited. Half were randomly assigned to an aerobic exercise program. "... The group doing aerobic exercise had increases in hippocampus volume: up to 2.12 percent in the left hippocampus and 1.97 percent in the right hippocampus. ... The group that didn't exercise saw a 1.4 percent *decrease* in hippocampus size." (27)

Osteoporosis

Another risk facing those with MS is osteoporosis, which is the loss of bone mass. The risk of breaking bones is greater in the presence of osteoporosis. While also affecting males, osteoporosis is a major health threat for aging females, affecting about 8 million of the 10 million osteoporosis sufferers in the U.S. One in three women over 50 get fractures resulting from osteoporosis. Another 34 million have osteopenia, a precursor of the disease. (28)

Furthermore, there are 300,000 hip fractures per year in the United States. According to Dr. Edward C. Geehr, MD, *Lifescript* Chief Medical Officer, "About 24 percent of hip-fracture patients and a third of elderly men with hip fractures die within a year, often because they can't regain mobility." (29)

One of the ways to ensure healthy bones and reduce the risk of fractures is strength training. Geehr recommends several ways to make and maintain healthy bones through strength training with weight-bearing exercises (such as walking, jogging and dancing). "These help prevent or slow the progression of osteoporosis. Strength training increases the tug of muscles on the bones and weight-bearing exercises also stresses bones, which keeps them strong. " (30)

Strength and flexibility training exercises may be done at home without expensive equipment. Lisa Reale Munn, a certified personal trainer and proponent of home-based exercise, said, 'It's super-important for women to incorporate resistance training into their weekly regimen to protect and strengthen their bones, as well as maintain and protect their bodies, organs and overall health." (31)

The risk of disability increases with normal aging due to loss of muscle and bone mass. Coupled with MS in the absence of strength training, the risk of falls and breaking of bones becomes even greater.

Strength and flexibility may be done at home. Carol walks up the stairs several times a day to our upstairs office. When walking up stairs, she lifts her thighs as high as possible in an exaggerated fashion, which strengthens the quadriceps and iliopsoas. Later in the book, I will show more strength training exercises that can be done in the home.

Supplements & Exercise

Based on studies conducted by Kristi Uusi-Rasi, a senior researcher at the UKK Institute for Health Promotion Research,

> Exercise and vitamin D supplements may help prevent injurious falls in older adults. Exercises, done regularly over two years, concentrated on balance, weight bearing, strength and agility. ... Neither vitamin D nor supplements nor exercise reduced the number of falls. But compared with the placebo without exercise group, those who took vitamin D alone were 16 percent less likely to be injured in a fall; the placebo and exercise groups were 54 percent less likely to be injured; and those who exercised and took supplements were 62 percent less likely to be hurt. ... Physical conditioning and vitamin D increase bone density, which could help prevent injury. (32)

Caregiving Needs and Concerns

Love bears all things, believes all things,
hopes all things, endures all things.
—1 Corinthians 13: 7, RSV

Through love, be servants of one another.
—Ephesians 5: 13 RSV

Given Carol's experience, we had become desperate. I experienced enormous stress. MS is a family disease and a heavy burden falls on the caregiver, often a spouse.

Peter Rosenberger, in an *AARP* article, stated that an estimated 65 million Americans already serve as volunteer caregivers for an elderly, chronically ill, or disabled love one. As Baby Boomers step into senior status, an increasing number of men and women are finding themselves facing difficult challenges in caring for vulnerable family members. "If you love someone, you'll eventually be a caregiver. If you live long enough, you'll need one." (33)

Rosenberger's wife had both legs amputated as a result of a car accident. He knew of her serious accident before they married. He writes,

> Caring for a disabled wife for three decades has taught me about America's healthcare system, life, love and faith. It's been quite a journey: 78 operations. Both of her legs amputated, treatment by 60+ doctors in 12 hospitals, $9 million in medical bills—and it's ongoing. We caregivers are, by definition, 'high-functioning multi-taskers' and it's often difficult for others to know how to help us. We seem to move at break-neck speeds and those who are caregivers just can't seem to keep up. (34)

In his article, entitled "I See You, Caregiver," Rosenberger continues. "I've learned that I serve my wife best, when I am in a healthy place—physically, emotionally, professionally and fiscally. I am powerless to alleviate her pain or her disabilities. But I've learned the greatest gift I can give her is a husband who is healthy, calmer, and yes, even joyful—all while staring at grim realities." (35)

Carol describes me, her caregiver, as a "juggler on a tightrope." It is easy to lose balance. The objects of life's difficulties are continuously being thrown at me—and us. I risk falling. Sometimes it feels like I'm doing these activities blindfolded. I am reminded of scripture where Paul writes, "... for we walk by faith not by sight." (2 Corinthians 5: 7).

Donna Steigleder, in her article, "Caregiving Perspective: The Many Faces of Care," breaks down the components of her caregiving to her husband Lynn, who has MS. "The physical care is pretty consistent in that I know in advance what I'm going to need to do for him and how to do it; however, those other 'care' needs are more unpredictable." (36)

In another article, "Caregiver Perspective: Screaming on the Inside," Steigleder describes needed competencies. The physical requirements include the ability to shift, pull, and shift the body weight of the loved one, emotional stamina, and the ability to put self in second place to meet the needs of the one being cared for. The competencies required include house maintenance, creativity, perseverance, loyalty and self-sacrificing love. (37)

Steigleder's caregiving burden is far heavier and more extreme than mine because her husband's disabilities are far more advanced than Carol's. However, she is with legions of other caregivers. She describes the emotional burden as follows: "Here is what I am screaming on the inside. *I CAN'T TAKE THIS ANYMORE. I WANT TO*

QUIT. I WANT TO WALK AWAY AND NEVER LOOK BACK. I JUST CAN'T FACE ANOTHER NIGHT OF NO SLEEP; ANOTHER DAY OF PAIN; ANOTHER MINUTE OF FRUSTRATION AND DISAPPOINT-MENT; ANOTHER FAILURE." (38)

She describes other emotional pains including feeling guilty, angry and scared. "And yet, I push through it all. I fuss and cuss in a room away from him to get the anger out. I smile and tell others we're doing fine." (39)

My experience is similar to Steigleder's. When Carol fell on the floor and I couldn't help her up, or when she pooped on the floor, I would go into a rant and sometimes cuss—but never at her. It is wrong to curse at someone. Yes, as a fallible human being, this preacher cusses when highly stressed, ranting at the situation.

Sometimes I lecture and overreact to her for not listening to me or to her own body. At table grace, I pray for her strength and safety and thank God for her. I tell her frequently how grateful I am to have her in my life. And I thank her for being herself many times during the day.

The ranting did not help either one of us. The reverse was true, When I ranted, it increased her stress. On Ash Wednesday, February 10, during Lent in 2016, I went on a "rant fast" for forty days. The idea of Lent is to focus on what we give up. Sometimes what we give up is trivial, such as not eating desserts. What we add is what is important. There were setbacks and relapses, but I kept at it, with gentle reminders from Carol. As of this writing, my ranting has virtually disappeared. While Carol and I still have stressors, our stress levels have dropped significantly. The changes we make should be important enough to last a lifetime.

In his book, *Being Mortal: Medicine and What Matters in the End*, Atul Gawande describes the loving bond between Felix, who has terminal cancer, and his wife Bella:

> She and Felix felt the sorrows of their losses but also the pleasures of what they still had. Although she might not have been able to remember me or others she didn't know too well, she enjoyed company and conversation and sought both out. Moreover, she and Felix still had their own, private, decades-long conversation that never stopped.

> He found great purpose in caring for her, and she, likewise, found great meaning in being there for him. The physical presence of each other gave them comfort. He dressed her, bathed her, helped feed her.

> When they walked, they held hands. At night, they lay in bed in each other's arms, awake and nestling for a while, before drifting off to sleep. These moments, Felix said, remained among their most cherished. He felt they knew each other, and loved each other more than at any time in their nearly seventy years together. (40)

I am reminded of a verse from *The Song of Solomon*, "This is my beloved, and this is my friend." (The Song of Solomon 5: 16)

In another book, *Healing the Soul: Unexpected Stories of Courage, Hope and the Power of Mind*, neurologist and MS specialist Bhupendra O. Khatri, MD, devotes an entire chapter to caregiving.

> Caregivers are also more prone to depression, physical ailments, and social isolation. They need psychological and emotional support, as well as time off periodically to prevent burnout. (41)

Khatri further notes,

> The gender of the partner who is ill makes a huge difference
> in the rates of divorce. The divorce rate for marriages in
> which the husband had MS was as low at 3 percent while
> nearly 21 percent of couples in which the wife had MS,
> ended in divorce.
>
> This is a significant finding since women are more often
> afflicted with the disease than men (four to one). Early signs
> of burnout include neglecting one's self, alcohol abuse, low
> threshold for losing one's temper, and insomnia.
>
> If these signs are recognized early, appropriate interven-
> tions can prevent many problems such as divorce and
> serious illness. (42)

Khatri describes how both the one with MS and his or her spouse
feel about each other. Gretchen has MS and describes how grateful
she is to have her husband Medrow in her life.

> Gretchen was tearful when she told me how fortunate she
> was to have Medrow. Without him, she would have been
> dead a long time ago, if not physically then, emotionally for
> sure. She has no words to describe her love and gratitude
> for her husband, except to say, 'He is my angel." (43)

The neurologist tells of Richard, who ultimately died from MS, and
his wife Judith.

> We both grew in our marriage and I truly experienced the
> 'marriage bliss' they talk about. To me it was an energy that
> elevated us far beyond physical and emotional love. Sure, it
> was tough at times; but as I look back, now that Richard is
> gone, I feel God placed me in the situation I was in. I would
> do it all over again. (44)

God is our refuge and strength,
a very present help in trouble.
—Psalms 41: 1 RSV

The Support of Friends and God's Help
God's help is often mediated by friends and sometimes by strangers. Carol and I get support in many ways. We have many friends with MS and their caregiver spouses. We call that circle of friends, "the church of the MS."

We also have support from our church family, Trinity Presbyterian Church in Nashville. On one occasion, Guy Hicks, an elder at the church and his wife, Marcie, came to our house and helped me get Carol off the floor. She has fallen many times at church, once in the sanctuary during worship. Strangers often are kind, frequently just opening doors for us. I always say to them, "That is kind." Other times, strangers may offer to help her to her feet if she falls. All this is our extended support system.

Caregiver Support Services
There are caregiver support services worth noting. One online service on Facebook is "The Caregiver Space." This is a place of comfort, relief and connection with other caregivers who understand. There are tabs for Community, Caregiver Stories, and The Caregiver Toolbox.

Another Facebook service is "The Fearless Caregiver." Peter Rosenberger posts there sometimes. Rosenberger is a radio talk show host focused on caregiving and broadcasting out of WLAC 1510 AM in Nashville Sundays at 3:00 pm Central Time. His program is also found on KGA in Spokane, WA and WMEX Boston, as well as iHeart Media. He hosts and speaks at numerous Fearless Caregiver Conferences across the country. He is author of the book,

Hope for the Caregiver, and I highly recommend visiting his webpage, www.caregivers-withhope.com.

I was a guest on his show September 15, 2015, entitled, "His Wife has MS. He has a Mission." You can listen to the broadcast at: peterrosenberger.podbean.com/2015/09/.

So, what did we do and what can be done?

Keep on reading!

* * * * *

Chapter 1 — Endnotes

(1)   "Multiple Sclerosis Patients Especially Sensitive to Heat," *Healthline News.*

(2)   Foley, Frederick W., PhD, "Intimacy and Sexuality with Multiple Sclerosis," Multiple Sclerosis Foundation, © Copyright 2000-2013, Multiple Sclerosis Foundation, www.msfocus.org.

(3)   Ibid.

(4)   Brody, Jane E., "The Far-Reaching Effects of a Fall," *The New York Times,* March 10, 2015.

(5)   Bemben, Michael G. PhD, "The physiology of aging: What you can do to slow or stop the loss of muscle mass – Research," *Aerobics and Fitness Association of America,* 2002 Gale Group, February 2001.

(6)   Kolaczkowski, Laura, "MS & Comorbidities," *Multiple Sclerosis.net,* June 10, 2015.

(7)   Dionyssiotis, Y., "Body composition in multiple sclerosis," US National Library of Medicine, National Institute of Health, *Hippokratia, Quarterly Medical Journal,* 2013 – Jan-Mar.

(8)   Hughes, Sue, "Obesity Linked to Increased Risk for MS," *Medscape,* March 12, 2014.

(9)   Kopman, Jeffrey, Staff Writer, "Obese Girls Much More Likely to Develop Multiple Sclerosis," Everyday Health, Last Updated 1/30/2013

(10) Patz, Aviva, "Coping with dual diagnoses," *Momentum*, Spring 2016.

(11) Smith, Claire, "Symptoms Involved in Ehlers-Danlos Syndrome Hypermobili-ty-Type and Joint Hypermobility Syndrome," Web-stat.com .

(12) Feinstein, Anthony, MD, "The Neuropsychiatry of Multiple Sclerosis," *Canadian Journal of Psychiatry*, March 2004.

(13) Fiore, Kristina, Staff Writer, *MedPage Today*, "MS Patients at Greater Risk of Suicide," *MedPage Today.*.

(14) WebMd, Reviewed by Rinku Chatterjee on February 20, 2012.

(15) National Multiple Sclerosis Society publication.

(16) Emrich, Lisa, *Heath Guide Tuesday*, March 24, 2009, www.healthcenter.com, "How to Manage MS Related Spasticity," Source: Spasticity, by Sue Kushner, MS, PT and Kathi Brandfass, MS, PT, Clinical Bulletin/Information for Health Professionals, © 2004, National Multiple Sclerosis Society.

(17) Chester, Cathy, "Everybody Loves A Hug, But Not MS Hugs. What Is An MS Hug?" MultipleSclerosis.net, August 24, 2013.

(18) Jongen, PI; Ter Horst AT; Brand AM, "Cognitive Impairment in multiple sclerosis," US National Library of Medicine, National Institute of Health, PubMed.gov.

(19) "Cognitive Changes," National MS Society.

(20) Juntti, Melaina, "Smoking Bad for the Brain, Too," *Men's Journal*, July 2013.

(21) The Expanded Disability Status Scale (EDSS) was developed by neurologist Dr. John F. Kurtzke in "Rating neurological impairment in multiple sclerosis: an expanded disability status scale, (EDSS), *Neurology* 1983 / 33 (11): 1444-52.

(22) *American Fitness*, May-June 2002.

(23) Matthews, Jessica, MS, E-RYT, Exercise Physiologist, American Council of Exercise, "Best Strength-Training Exercises for Women," *Lifescript Healthy Living for Women*, 3/21/2012.

(24) "Hormones and gender under the microscope," *Momentum*, Fall 2014.

(25) Reynolds, Gretchen, "To Age Well, Walk," *New York Times*, May 27, 2014.

(26) Ibid.

(27) "Exercise: A Simple Way to Radically Increase Your Brain Power," *Fitness Peak*, Mercola.com, March 7, 2011.

(28) Geehr, Edward C., MD, Lifescript Chief Medical Officer, "7 Tips For Healthy Bones If You're over 30," *Lifescript Healthy Living For Women*, 12/20/2014

(29) Ibid.

(30) Ibid.

(31)   Munn, Lisa Reale, "Resistance Training at Home," *The Tennessean*, January 9, 2014.

(32)   Bakalar, Nicholas, "Ways to Prevent Injuries in Falls," *New York Times*, March 31, 2015.

(33)   Rosenberger, Peter, "I See You, Caregiver," AARP TN.

(34)   Ibid.

(35)   Ibid.

(36)   Steigleder, Donna, "Caregiving Perspective: The Many Faces of Care," Multiple Sclerosis.net, March 3, 2015

(37)   Ibid.

(38)   Steigleder, Donna, "Caregiver Perspective: Screaming on the Inside," Multiple Sclerosis.net, July 25, 2015

(39)   Ibid.

(40)   Gawande, Atul, MD, *Being Mortal, Medicine and What Matters in the End*, Metropolitan Books, Henry Holt and Company, New York, p. 56

(41)   Khatri, Bhupendra O., MD, *Healing The Soul, Unexpected Stories of Courage, Hope, and the Power of Mind*, HenschelHAUS Publishing , Milwaukee, WI,.

(42)   Ibid.

(43)   Ibid.

(44)   Ibid.

CHAPTER 2
WHAT WE DID TO REVERSE MS

What does not kill me makes me stronger.
—Friedrich Nietzsche, *Twilight of the Idols,* 1888

Where there is no struggle, there is no strength.
—Oprah Winfrey

When I worked as a chaplain at Middle Tennessee Mental Health Institute in Nashville, the Clinical Director said, "Patients are responsible for their illnesses." This does not mean the patient caused the illness. In healthy and functional relationships with doctors and other health-care professionals, the patient and provider work together as a team. I believe that is true for Carol and for anyone with any disease. The patient is responsible for his or her illness.

In my years of playing college football in the early sixties, I learned a great deal about strength training. A basic assumption is that heavy weights and lower repetitions create more muscle mass than lower weights and higher repetitions.

When we began, we started our work-out regimen at home. Carol held on to a hand rail for balance and did simple squats, strengthening the quadriceps. To strengthen the calf muscles, she also did calf raises with the balls of her feet on a 2-by-4-inch board. (Please refer to the Addendum at the end of the book regarding appropriate number of repetitions, etc.)

After we had been doing these simple set of exercises, she had a follow-up examination with her neurologist. On exam, the doctor pressed his hand against her thigh while she lifted her thigh against the pressure of his hand. This tests the strength of the iliopsoas. Suddenly, the doctor jerked his head back in surprise. He asked what she had been doing. We told him she had been doing strength training.

Carol and I proceeded with some basic assumptions. I assumed patients were responsible for their illnesses. A basic hypothesis is that muscle mass will make up for some of the deficits in the central nervous system. I assumed that we would create muscle mass with an aggressive course of strength and flexibility training from neck to feet. I assumed that we must listen to our bodies; our bodies do not lie. I assumed we must "do no harm," an essential tenant of medicine.

I shared my basic hypothesis that an increase in muscle mass would make up for some of the neurological deficits in MS patients with a neurologist at an MS-specific dinner sponsored by a pharmaceutical company. He said, "That isn't right." I was confounded by his response and said something to the effect that he had stopped being a scientist, since science is driven by curiosity. In retrospect, I would have asked, "Where is the scientific evidence to support that assertion?"

I further assume all exercises are not created equal when it comes to creating muscle mass and that strength training is the preferred form of exercise, in contrast to aerobic exercise, yoga, or stretching alone for those with MS. As noted earlier, 70 percent of those with MS are heat sensitive, so aerobic exercise would not be indicated for them. The downside for aerobic training is that for someone with MS, body temperature will rise causing the legs and arms to turn into liquid Jello.

Many of those with MS choose to partake in water exercise. Water aerobics do not create muscle mass, but free-style swimming, back stroke, and breast stroke do—however, not to the same extent as strength training.

Bike riding may increase muscle mass in the quadriceps and calves and is good for the cardiovascular system, but becoming overheated needs to be taken into consideration. Nor does bike riding create muscle mass in the other major muscle groups. For those with MS, bike riding might be considered in an air-conditioned gym.

Walking is always a good choice, preferably in an air-conditioned environment.

Cognition, Memory and Exercise

Multiple studies indicate that strength training helps cognitive function in aging adults. Walking appears to help memory in older adults. Also, researchers studied women ages 70 to 80 with mild cognitive impairment (MCI) who were divided into one of three groups: strength training, aerobic exercise, and balance and tone training. At the end of the study, it was found that those who participated in resistance training fared best. They outperformed the other groups on measuring attention, memory and higher-order brain functions like conflict resolution. They also showed improvement in brain regions involved in memory. (1)

Other studies found similar results. Researchers Nagamatsu, Handy, Hsu, Voss, and Liu-Ambrose, state, "Our study suggests that twice-weekly RT is a promising strategy to alter the trajectory of cognitive decline in seniors with mild cognitive impairment."(2)

Numerous studies are finding that strength training is able to give a boost to seniors' brains. As both aging and MS progress, the risk to cognitive functions grows over time. One study focused on women between 70 and 80 years old who complained of memory difficulties and were deemed to have "probable" MCI. One third of the women were randomly assigned to a strength training program that included lifting weights, one third walked outdoors in an aerobics program, and one third took basic balance and toning classes.

> After 6 months compared to those in the balance/tone classes, the strength training group was found to have achieved "significant" cognitive improvement. The strength training group also experienced activity changes in three specific parts of the brain's cortex associated with cognitive behavior, the researchers found. These changes were not seen among the balance/tone group. (3)

One of the important cognitive functions affected by MS is memory. Almost 60 percent of people with MS experience some sort of memory problems, according to the National Multiple Sclerosis Society. More rarely, in 5 to 10 percent of people with MS, memory becomes so limited that it significantly interferes with daily function. (4)

The risk of developing secondary progressive MS increases with age, even in the absence of new brain or spinal lesions. A well-known neurologist and MS researcher at Vanderbilt University, indicates there is a 50-percent chance that there will disease progression even with disease-modifying drugs. (5)

Strength training holds promise to delay or even reverse disability due to MS. In the brain, the hippocampus is linked to the limbic system, which includes the hypothalamus, and impacts sexual function, endocrine function, behavioral function, and autonomic control. Much has been written on brain function and MS; this goes beyond the scope of this book.

Exercise—Carol and I believe strength training in particular—creates positive changes in the brain. The relevance and how this worked for Carol will be described later.

The Road to Reversing MS Disability

Carol's disabilities took a U-Turn on January 2, 2012, which was when we began an aggressive course of strength and flexibility training, with me as her trainer, at a local YMCA. We are grateful for the Y and its staff. Members look and sound like America. There are whites, blacks, Hispanics, Asians, and people from the Middle East. Some of the women wear the hijab. We are surrounded by a multiplicity of languages other than English.

After the first exercise session, Carol was so fatigued that she placed her head on the table and fell asleep at the Y's snack bar. One of the staff was so concerned that he asked Carol what was wrong. Walking back to the car, she was so weak she had to sit at a chair on the Y porch before resuming her trek.

Despite the initial fatigue and weakness, Carol noticed positive results within a week. In the coming weeks and months, we continued the exercise regime by increasing the amount of weight with free weights and resistance machines.

Workout Rationale

Our workout rationale is based on four assumptions. First, the brain and the body, including the muscle-skeletal system, is an integrated system. Everything works together. Therefore, arms, core, legs, and ankles must all be strengthened with flexibility training included. Arms and core are important for balance, and, in the event of a fall, are critical to getting back to one's feet.

Second, when a particular sub-system is worked, it is important to work all the muscle groups. For instance, in exercising the quads and calves, it is important to work the abductors and adductors, as well as the ankles.

Third, balance and coordination are influenced by many muscle groups, where muscle mass and muscle strength play key roles. Evidence already cited indicates that people who do strength training do better than those who only do aerobics, balance and toning exercises.

Fourth, the smooth muscles that control bladder and bowel functions must be strengthened as well. This requires the consistent incorporation of Kegel exercises into the exercise routine. Each time we do floor exercises, Carol does 40 Kegel contractions of her bladder and bowel sphincters. She also does these on days we don't work out while I drive the car.

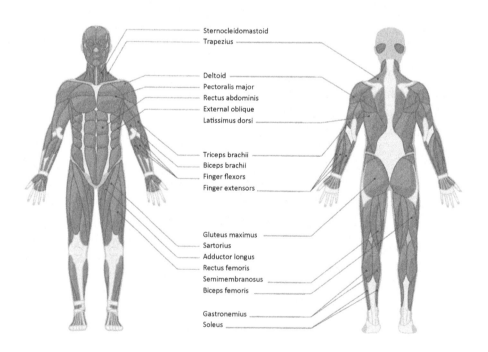

Sternocleidomastoid
Trapezius
Deltoid
Pectoralis major
Rectus abdominis
External oblique
Latissimus dorsi
Triceps brachii
Biceps brachii
Finger flexors
Finger extensors
Gluteus maximus
Sartorius
Adductor longus
Rectus femoris
Semimembranosus
Biceps femoris
Gastronemius
Soleus

Strength Gains

The gains in strength, as measured in the amount of weight pushed, have been enormous for her. Those gains in strength are evidenced in multiple matrices, described in the next section.

During all workouts, we drink ice water. Water is needed for hydration. Ice water is needed to cool the body through the core. A set of exercises does increase body temperature, while ice water brings the temperature down. Also, I do my exercises between Carol's reps, which allows her body temperature to recede on its own.

On Sundays and Tuesdays in the early afternoon, we work arms and core with back extensions, dead lifts and abdominal crunches. On Tuesday mornings, Carol works out with a professional trainer for a half hour. He donates his time pro bono with a group composed mostly of people with MS and one woman who has cerebral palsy. This is the trainer's way of giving back out of his Christian faith motivation.

On Mondays and Wednesdays, we do legs and core. On Fridays, we make up any body work we might have missed due to schedule conflicts. We keep a "Strength Workout Record" each time we work out and note "high-water marks" for each exercise when one is reached. For example, when Carol is able to do 20 reps on a given exercise, we move up the weight being pushed by 5 pounds. Even as recently as November 15, 2016, she matched or reached new high-water marks on three exercises. On November 16, she matched or exceeded six out of nine high-water marks. And on November 27, she matched one high-water mark and achieved two new high-water marks. Amazing!

To begin with, the exercises were a combination of exercise machines, dumbbells and barbells, with me spotting her on the machines and free weights. These days, we do mostly exercise machines, since they are easier and safer to use. We use dumbbells only on concentration curls and lateral raises. We use a 20-pound barbell on the dead lift. We do three sets of each exercise except for the dead lift, where we do one set. On the dead lift, I spot her and make sure she is steady. We do three sets unless she experiences excessive fatigue, then we scale it back to one or two sets, but this is rare.

We always listen to her body. The body does not lie. We must understand the message the body is giving and not ignore it. If Carol experiences sharp pain during an exercise, then we stop. If she experiences a cramp during a stretching exercise, we ease off until the cramp loosens, and then we resume.

There is a difference between a sharp pain versus the "burn" of muscle fatigue, which builds as muscles tire after a number of reps.

After a 20-minute rest, we always finish with floor and standing stretching exercises following strength training exercises.

In December 2014, we also added Pilates, which strengthens the core, to our stretching regimen.

Together, Carol and I totaled 8 hours of exercise a week as she continued to reverse disabilities and restore lost functions. Since early 2015, we have scaled back to about half that to maintain gains. As the saying goes, "If you don't use it, you lose it." This appears to be working.

Our first existing Strength Workout Record is dated April 12, 2012, which reflected gains from January 2, 2012, but that record can't be found. Some of the differences are due to the Y's dropping the lateral press machine, so we switched to dumbbells. We now do mostly exercise machines, because they are easier and safer for us to use, and we no longer do bench presses.

However, gains in strength as measured by weight pushed is noteworthy:

- Lateral Pull Down: On 4/5/12 was 45 pounds and 17 reps, representing a high-water mark.
- Chest Press: On 4/5/12 was 15 pounds and 7 reps. On 11/30/14, it was 40 pounds and 13 reps.
- Seated Bicep Curls: On 4/5/12 went from went from 5 pounds and 14 reps to Concentration Curls on 5/6/16 to 12 pounds and 14 reps.
- Abdominal Crunches went from 30 pounds and 13 reps on 4/5/12 to 57 pounds and 13 reps on 3/21/16.
- Back Extensions went from went from 75 pounds and 30 reps and one set on 4/5/12 to 130 pounds and 20 reps on 2/15/16. We added the Arm Extension machine, which works the triceps. On 4/10/16 on the Arm Extension she did 50 pounds and 16 reps.

Similar results were obtained on the leg exercises.

- On the Leg Press machine, Carol went from 245 pounds and 20 reps on 4/9/12 to 425 pounds and 11 reps on 12/3/14.
- Seated Leg Curls went from 45 pounds and 30 reps on 4/9/12 to 95 pounds and 14 reps on 5/9/16.
- Standing Calf Raises went from 10 pounds and 10 reps on 4/9/12 to a Seated Calf Press with 95 pounds and 16 reps on 2/17/16.
- The Seated Hip Adduction, which works the inner thighs, went from 60 pounds and 20 reps on 4/9/12 to 85 pounds and 16 reps on 5/9/16.
- The Seated Hip Abduction went from 35 pounds and 20 reps on 4/9/12 to 85 pounds and 17 reps on 5/23/16.

It is worth noting that Carol could not lift her legs over the pads on the exercise machines without my assistance at the beginning. She simply did not have enough strength in her iliopsoas muscle. The iliopsoas muscle lifts the thigh from either a sitting or standing position. Now she can lift her legs over the pads every time without my assistance. This is due to her having stronger iliopsoas.

On March 30, 2014 we added the Leg Lift Machine to the routine to work the iliopsoas. Carol does leg lifts with her legs bent at the knees and her forearms on the pads. At the beginning, she could not lift herself into position with her forearms on the pads. She can now get into position with ease. She does 4 sets of 9 to 11 reps.

The results were seen that first day in that Carol could get her legs into her pants with greater ease. She could also lift her legs into the car without difficulty. In addition, she can move her foot from the accelerator to the brake more easily, which makes driving safer.

Flexibility Gains

Carol and I do two levels of flexibility exercises from neck to feet following strength training and a 20-minute break to rehydrate and rest.

When we began floor exercises, it was often a struggle for Carol to get back to her feet, even using the hand rail next to her floor mat. Early on, I noticed she could not point her feet up while lying down, indicating foot drop.

We do a full set of floor exercises followed by standing exercises, holding each stretch for 30 seconds. Following the floor exercises, Carol does 30 contractions of Kegel exercises, alternately contracting and relaxing her bowel and bladder sphincters.

On days we don't work out, she does Kegels while we drive in the car and every night at bedtime, lying in bed before going to sleep. Along with the medicines, this has been pivotal in gaining control of her bladder and bowel functions.

We finish part of the floor routine with me holding her feet as she does isometric pressure against the pressure of my hands in three directions. This has eliminated foot drop and foot cramps. We do three sets for a 40-second count.

Multiple Clinical Gains Reversing Disability

For Carol, there have been multiple clinical gains affecting many areas of disability and restoring multiple functions. Our quality of life has improved significantly and my stress is less. The ability to walk longer distances before fatigue has improved dramatically. Also, Carol can lift her legs to a two-foot rail when she exercises with a personal trainer, which is something she could not do previously.

As mentioned above, Carol has gained control over bladder and bowel functions. There have not been any more episodes of projectile pooping, and only rare and minor episodes of peeing on herself, and those only when she has had a urinary tract infection. Besides Kegels, the full regimen for controlling bladder and bowel functions includes a prescription for trospium chloride; an over-the-counter stool softener; psyllium fiber capsules or Metamucil; and two fingers high of prune juice at breakfast.

Other risks for loss of bladder control occur when she needs to have a bowel movement due to the pressure on her bladder. After a bowel movement and after she stands up, she may then pee. She can go much longer periods of time before needing to urinate.

While Carol still falls, she does so less frequently and is less likely to injure herself. In July 2015, she had six falls. Once she fell into the Adduction/Abduction machine at the Y and needed help to extricate herself. In May 2016, she fell in the hallway at the Y, which left a bruise on her chin. All the Y staff were very concerned and helpful.

She did have one hard fall in which she was knocked unconscious. Having forgotten her walker, she only had her cane and on October 29, 2014, she fell face-forward at the entrance to a restaurant. She cut her forehead as well and had to be taken to the ER. The CT scan was negative and she was released.

Carol also fell on December 22, 2014 and again, was knocked unconscious when her head struck the floor in our home. After gaining consciousness, she was able to get up and sit in a chair. Metro ambulance was called. When they arrived, one of the EMTs did a mental status exam, which showed that her short-term memory was impaired. She could not name the President, the date and could not remember how she fell. The responder also ruled out that I had caused her to fall.

Once, when walking on the sidewalk at a local mall, Carol fell as she was walking over a grate. Anything can be a "road hazard." Fortunately, in this case, "no harm, no foul."

When Carol does fall, she almost always can get up on her own without assistance. At other times, especially when she has a urinary tract infection, she may have more difficulty getting up. Generally, when she falls, because of the strength training, it is easier for Carol to get up as she has greater strength is her arms, core and legs.

An additional benefit of strength training and other exercise is that Carol's range of motion in her right arm improved to the point that she can now reach the top of her head with her right hand, which she was unable to do before (after the dislocation of her right shoulder and completion of physical therapy). This helps with many activities of daily living, such as being able to pull the door handle on the passenger side of the car. From the driver's side of the car, Carol can now reach over to the glove compartment, which she could not do previously. At home, when she is seated at the bathroom counter next to the sink, she can reach to a shelf for her pill containers, which was not possible before.

The Seated Vertical Press has contributed to that improvement. This machine strengthens the deltoids (shoulder muscles). Also, the Lateral Raise with dumbbells strengthens the deltoids and trapezium, which are next to the deltoids toward the back of the neck. However, her shoulder injury still means Carol can't wipe herself from behind after a bowel movement, so I wipe her with a warm, wet washcloth.

Carol never has cramping in her feet. Spasticity only happens rarely the day after her Betaseron shot. She may have flu-like symptoms, problems with balance and walking after the shot. With strength training, her walking is not as stiff-legged and more normal and her legs are not stiff as boards. In addition to Baclofen, we attribute these improvements to our regimen of strength and flexibility training.

Also, Carol has shown improvement in the strength and dexterity in her hands and fingers. We attribute that to gripping the bars during strength training, as this strengthens the forearms and hands. Also, we invested in a medium-resistance Grip Master, which she uses on a daily basis and strengthens individual fingers. One gain is that she can now push down on the button the hair mousse dispenser, which she could not do previously. She also observed that at a meal, she could cut up her food more easily.

A further improvement is that Carol has been able to rise from the toilet seat without using the grab bar or from a chair or sofa without pushing up with her arms. She can now rise from a rocking chair without assistance. She sits in a rocker when reading to young children at a local community center.

Another gain is that she can walk upstairs more easily and has a more upright posture. When she walks upstairs, she does an exaggerated left lift to further strengthen the illipsoas. The improvement in posture is the result of greater back strength from the Back Extension Machine and the Pilates program we do during our flexibility session.

Also, she can transfer from bed to toilet at night without falling. She has not had any falls at night since these physical improvements.

It is worth noting that core strengthening is important for those with MS. According to neurophysiotherapist Margaret Gear and Dr. Jenny Freeman of the MS Research Group, studies have shown that people with MS can have significantly reduced balance even when they have no problem walking. (6)

> People with MS have been found to have reduced stability during arm movements and individuals with delayed activation of trunk muscles have reduced balance. ...

> The exercises were progressed as mobility improved. Participants also did 15 minutes of these same exercises at home each day. ...

> There was variability in how the participants responded to the core stability training. Five people clearly benefited with improvement in seven of the nine measures. These showed improved walking speed, better balance, reaching forward and to the side, improved balance while standing on one leg, and less difficulty carrying a drink while walking. One further participant gained some benefit, in four of the measures, while two people did not appear to gain any benefit. (7)

Bone Density Improvement

Strength training has also paid off with apparent strengthening of Carol's bone mass. She began taking Fosamax for osteopenia upon diagnosis by her endocrinologist. Osteopenia refers to bone density that is lower than normal peak density, but not low enough to be classified as osteoporosis. She was on Fosamax for five or six years and went off the drug in 2007. Carol's osteopenia was under control and bone mass was within normal limits.

At her most recent examination on July 31, 2014, her bone density was well within normal limits in spite of being off medication for seven years. Upon seeing the bone density screening results, her doctor exclaimed, "Wow!" He attributes her normal bone density to her strength training over the prior two years. The stronger the bones, the less likely she will have a fracture in the event of a fall.

Improvement in Fatigue Levels

In the past, Carol would have to take a nap after exercising, but only rarely does she now need to take a nap after exercise.

Improvement in Near Vision, Sense of Smell

Another interesting development was an improvement in Carol's near vision. She uses contact lenses, but wears reading glasses for near vision. Upon examination by her optometrist on July 23, 2014, he said her near vision had improved and she no longer needed reading glasses. When I asked my ophthalmologist about this, he said cataracts could improve near vision. Carol doesn't have cataracts.

Coupled with near vision, her sense of smell improved as well. She has increased ability in her olfactory system.

Resurrection of Carol's Libido & Mood

The most amazing change has been the resurrection of Carol's libido. Over the prior ten years, she experienced the decline of sexual capacity, including sexual pleasure and orgasmic ability. Her vagina did not naturally lubricate so we used a water-soluble lubricant if I wanted sex. She did not initiate sex, nor was she interested in it. She came to believe she would never again experience orgasm, and was saddened and even despaired at that prospect.

Beginning on January 12, 2014 and very rapidly on January 18th, she began again to notice a return of sexual pleasure and the ability to achieve orgasm. The first indication something was happening was when she started to have erotic dreams to the point of climax.

Before these changes, we rated her interest in sex as a 3 on a 10-point scale. On the 18th, her interest moved rapidly to a 10. To use a metaphor, Carol was revived from a "near-death" experience of her sexuality.

The link between exercise and libido is documented in an evidence-based study.

> New research confirms that women who exercise have a better time in bed. In a study from the University of Texas at Austin, women with low sex drives (caused by prescription drugs) who worked out regularly for 21 days reported higher sexual desire—especially when they had sex after a workout. Their exercise-related improvement in genital blood flow is probably a result women not on meds can also expect. (8)

This has certainly been the case with Carol. When this happened early on, her libido was very high and we would frequently have sex after a workout. As of this writing, that is not quite as true.

Treatment of orgasmic loss in women with MS has been poorly studied, and I contend, should be the topic of further study.

Coupled with this change in her sex drive, Carol's mood improved. She has never been depressive, but her mood shifted from a 7 to 10 without evidence of mania.

Testosterone Levels

Amazingly, Carol's total testosterone level went to 670.9 ng/dl on lab results of July 29, 2014. This was even though at age 68, she was post-menopausal. Her primary care physician responded by commenting that her testosterone level was higher than his as a normal middle-aged male. Testosterone levels in women vary. According to the University of Rochester Medical Center, normal measurements range from 17 to 70 ng/dl.

Carol's neurologist expressed surprise when told of those lab results. Subsequent lab results showed her testosterone levels dropping to 352.2 ng/dl on December 1, 2014 and 184.6 ng/dl on March 29, 2015. Then her testosterone went back up to 375.0 ng/dl on August 4, 2015. On January 31, 2016, it was measured at 250.3 ng/dl. The last reading on August 15, 2016, it measured 46.3 ng/dl. This last number is above average for pre-menopausal women and well above the average in post-menopausal women.

Carol is not as horny as she was when her testosterone levels were so much higher. However, she still lubricates well and reminds me what to do when I get a nocturnal erection. We now describe our relationship as a healthy and equal balance of *eros* (sexual love), *agape* (self-sacrificing love), and *phila* (friendship love). We are a happy and joyous mix of friends and lovers, and truly are BFFs, best friends forever.

She is a changed women and I love it. So does she!

Androgens

In a woman's body, one of the main purposes of androgens, male hormones, is to be converted into female hormones called estrogens. Women typically produce low levels of male hormones (androgens) in the ovaries, adrenal glands and fat cells. Women's androgen levels drop after entering menopause. Excess androgen levels in a woman's blood stream can cause obvious physical effects (9), including:

♦ infertility
♦ loss of scalp hair
♦ acne
♦ irregular or absent menses
♦ growth of facial hair

At first, when Carol experienced the sexual changes, she was very sexually aroused daily. This was coupled with increased vaginal lubrication upon arousal. There is no longer any need for a water-soluble lubricant. She was and remains highly orgasmic. We have sex once to three times a week. She says she liked me a lot before these changes, but likes me even more now. I tell her that I'm even better looking now.

A side effect of the return of Carol's sexuality has been excessive hair growth on her face, neck, body and legs, as well as a loss of scalp hair on her forehead and the crown of her head. The hair is not dark and coarse as is typical of hirsutism, but dark and soft. (10)

As noted above, the pituitary gland stimulates hair growth with the follicle-stimulating hormone (FSH). An optimal FSH is 3.5-12.5. On the lab report of July 29, 2014, Carol's FSH was 41.7, well over the optimal upper limit. This increased to 42.0 on December 1, 2014 and by August 4, 2015, it had dropped to 41.4. It appears that the elevated FSH has caused the excessive hair growth. Carol has been having her facial hair removed with laser treatment. This is a condition we can live with. I kid her about growing bald and having a beard and she just grins in response.

Carol and I maintain that there is a link between exercise—strength training in particular—and the limbic system and the improvement in short-term vision, olfaction, bone mass, and libido, and is the result of the strength training we did, and continue to do.

Weight Loss

One of the collateral benefits in the resurrection of Carol's libido is that it became the motivating force in her losing weight. Motivation to do anything positive or change hinges on the *why*. For her, the *why* was the link between *feeling* sexy and *looking* slimmer and sexier. The *how* of change follows a compelling *why*.

Part of losing weight is accomplished by creating more muscle mass—which we did through strength training. Muscle mass is needed to burn more calories and fat, even when not exercising. Rarely does exercise alone lead to weight loss unless the person is a triathlete or other long-distance runner.

In addition, losing weight involves reducing total calories and the type of calories consumed. Most diets don't work, in that when people diet, their metabolism slows down. It is nature's way of protecting the species from the prospect of famine and starvation. Further, most or all of the weight that is lost most usually returns. The key to permanent weight loss is to change the number of calories consumed without feeling deprived.

Aaron Carroll believes that diet, not exercise alone, is crucial to weight loss. As an example, if an overweight man consumes 1,000 more calories than he is burning and wants to be in energy balance, he can do it by exercising. However, exercise burns far fewer calories than most people think. Thirty minutes of jogging or swimming laps might burn off 350 calories. People could achieve the same calorie reduction by eliminating two 16-ounce sodas each day. (11)

Many people think of dieting as a drastic and rigid change with the risk of putting the pounds back on, known as yo-yo dieting. Gradual changes in lifestyle and food choices mean losing weight in a more sustainable way.

For Carol and me, the key to weight loss was consuming more fresh veggies, fruit, protein and fewer carbohydrates. We cut calories and carbs, except in the morning, when she had Brie cheese on a muffin or biscuit. We also reduced our sugar consumption, which meant few or no desserts. This regimen resulted in weight loss for both of us and also demonstrates that it is easier to do this as a couple.

In October 2010, Carol weighed 200 pounds but had gotten down to 187. We started losing weight January 30, 2014. By July 30, 2016, she weighed 147 pounds for a total loss of 53 pounds. By October 8, 2016, she weighed 140 pounds, for a total weight loss of 60 pounds. As of this writing, Carol weighs 146 pounds, which is what she weighed when we married.

My weight dropped from 165 to 160 pounds and as of this writing, I weigh 150 pounds. In my senior year of high school, I played football at 168 pounds.

Her weight loss has been commented on by other members at the Y. On March 2, 2014, a Y member said, "You've lost weight." A friend whose wife has MS and also works out at the Y said, "You look as skinny as a pencil."

One of the collateral benefits of the weight loss for Carol has been going through her clothes closet and finding more fashionable and smaller-sized clothing. She is like a kid in a candy store. It is like shopping for clothes without spending any money. She feels more attractive as she has continued to lose weight.

Beyond that, if she falls to the floor, Carol can get up on her own without assistance, which is something she could not do earlier. She did have one hard fall in June 2016, landing on the right side of her face in the hallway to the bedroom. She said she was simply trying to move too fast. Carol received a gash over her right eye and broke a bone in the lower part of her eye socket, which caused her nose to bleed. She did not want to go to the emergency room to have the cut over her right eye sutured. Carol can be stubborn at times.

The next day, she had a major shiner on her right eye. We went to an MS luncheon sponsored by a pharma company. From there, we went to the ER, where a doctor confirmed the break. The exam suggested that the bone would heal on its own with no need for surgery.

Carol continues to have falls, some more severe than others. We recently went to see a documentary film with Q&A at Lipscomb University. It was very cold in the auditorium and the Q&A went on for some time. Carol is just as sensitive to cold as she is to heat, and needs to be in the sweet spot of ambient heat—not too cold, not too hot, but just right. By the time we left, Carol was shivering and her teeth were chattering. The following day, she fell four times; each time, we were able to get her up, either by myself or with the help of a friend. This reminded us of the bad old days when we had to call the fire department to help get her to her feet.

All things considered, we are very happy with this reversal of disabilities and return of lost functions.

The Many Benefits

Obviously, Carol and I are very happy with this turn of events. The questions is, can our approach be replicated by others?

One study cited by Amy Norton, *HealthDay* reporter, found positive results with stem-cell therapy for cases of relapsing MS, but not when it had become secondary progressive MS, or if the person had any form of MS for more than ten years. (12) Carol's MS is secondary progressive and has lasted more than ten years.

As far as my own research has revealed, I could not find anyone who had any form of progressive MS lasting ten or more years and showed a reversal of disability as Carol has. Of course, we can't say that anyone who follows our journey will experience the same improvement in olfaction, vision and sexuality. Certainly, more needs to be learned. A larger observational study with a greater selection of subjects should be conducted.

Carol continues to see progress in multiple ways, as others have observed. While there may be an occasional person in a wheelchair at the Y, she is the only person using a walker who consistently works out, which makes her highly visible when we work out on the fitness floor. When we exercise, people often comment on her improvement. She is often told by others that she is an inspiration to them. When she meets people who have not seen her for a while, they frequently comment on how good she looks. When she got a haircut, the owner of the shop who hadn't seen her in several months volunteered that she looked wonderful. One of her buddies in the exercise class led by her personal trainer told her that she could see an improvement in her posture. One couple at the Y told her they want to be just like us when they get older. On a visit with her neurologist, just looking at her and without further examination, he asked what she had been doing. We again told him she had been doing strength training. Carol's gains are noticeable to others.

Life is good and so is the sex.

Chapter 2—Endnotes

(1)   Sifferlin, Alexandra, "Mind Your Reps: Exercise, Especially Weight Lifting Helps Keep the Brain Sharp," Time, July 16, 2012.

(2)   Nagamatsu, Lindsey, MS; Handy, Todd C., PhD; :Hsu, C. Liang, BSc; Voss, Michelle, PhD; Liu-Ambrose, Teresa, PT; PhD; "Resistance training promotes cognitive and functional brain plasticity in seniors with mild cognitive impairment: a 6-month randomized clinical trial," PMC, US National Library of Medicine, National Institute of Health, *PubMed Central Canada*, April 23, 2012, 172(8), 666-668.

(3)   Moses, Alan, Health Day Reporter, "Strength Training May Give Boost to Seniors' Brains," *Health Day, US News*, 4/23/2012.

(4)   "12 Ways to Improve Memory with MS," Everyday Health.com, 2014.

(5)   Swenson, Rand; PT, MD, PhD; Dartmouth Medical School, Editor, Chapter 9, Limbic System, *Review of Clinical and Functional Neuroscience,* 2006.

(6)   Gear, Margaret, Neurophysiotherapist; Freeman, Jenny, Dr.; Reader in Physiotherapy, in "Core stability training in MS," Open Door – February 2011, pages 8-9, Multiple Sclerosis Trust, 2004 - 2013.

(7)   Ibid.

(8)   "Heat Up Her Cooldown," *Men's Health*, April 2014, p. 40.

(9)   Severson, Alexia; Barclay, Sam R.; "Testosterone Levels by Age," *Healthline*, Medically Reviewed by Steven Kim, MD on March 23, 2015.

(10)   Habif, TP, "Hair Diseases." In Habif, TP, ed., *Clinical Dermatology*, 5th Ed, St. Louis, MO, Mosby Elsevier, 3009, Chapter 24, *Medicine Plus*.

(11)   Carroll, Aaron E., "Diet, Not Exercise is Crucial to Weight Loss," *New York Times*, June 18, 2015.

(12)   Norton, Amy, HealthDay Reporter, "Early Study Says Stem Cells May Reverse Multiple Sclerosis Disability," Jan 20, 2015 *HealthDay*.

CHAPTER 3
WHAT YOU CAN DO

What, then, might anyone with MS do to take control and improve the quality of his or her life? Remember, an important assumption is that patients are responsible for their illness. If you have MS, you are responsible for your illness and do this in collaboration with your doctor and caregiver.

The previous chapters describe in detail the actions Carol and I did to reverse her disability and improve our quality of life. Of course, we cannot promise someone else will get the same results. On the other hand, you likely will find it is worth the effort. As the Nike slogan goes, "Just do it."

Strength Training and Primary Progressive MS

People with primary progressive MS, PPMS, are often told by their doctors that disease-modifying drugs will not help them. Or, if they have that diagnosis, even if a disease-modifying drug is prescribed, insurance companies will deny coverage. In some cases, the neurologist must argue for it to be approved. That can be disheartening. PPMS does not typically present with relapses. Rather, PPMS presents with a persistent and relentless increase in disability and loss of functions. Sometimes there may be attacks, but no remission.

I realize that strength training is not a cure for MS. Nor is there any cure for MS at this time. On the other hand, what would happen if someone with PPMS embarked on a strength and flexibility program as we did? Would there be at least the possibility of slowing the progression of disability?

Peggy Min is a dear friend of ours. She attends Trinity Presbyterian Church with us. She and her mother were both diagnosed with PPMS about the same time. Her mother eventually died due to complications from the disease. Peggy is quadriplegic because of her MS. She is bedridden and confined to a wheelchair. She can eat, move her head, talk and move her electric wheelchair with her chin or be pushed by a caregiver. She effectively uses a voice-activated computer.

Peggy is very active and attends church on a regular basis, where she is also an elder. Beyond that, she actively volunteers with me on Thursdays, joining me in a religious study group with men on death row at a local prison. She is an inspiration to both inmates and staff. During the Christmas season, she also participates in caroling at the prison.

A documentary film was made of Peggy by Demetria Kalodimos, the evening news anchor at WSMV, the NBC affiliate in Nashville, with me as a producer. Demetria was the executive producer, director, and editor. The five-minute short feature appeared on the Neuro Film Festival and can be viewed on YouTube under "Fearless: Peggy Min Faces MS."

Peggy does do isometric exercises by tightening and relaxing muscles and is guided in this by a physical therapist. She has regained some strength in her core, as evidenced by her ability to slightly move her trunk. Peggy believes very strongly that if she had followed an aggressive course of strength training earlier, she might have been able to slow the progression of her disease. This is anecdotal and should be the subject of an observational study.

Beyond that, there is nothing to prevent someone with PPMS from embarking on his or her own strength training program. This is especially true when people with progressive forms of MS are routinely told by their neurologists that there is nothing that can be done to slow the progression of disability. Remember, patients are responsible for their illness.

I conducted a systematic search for literature aimed at studies linking disease progression to exercise. As of this writing, I have not been able to find any research that determines if strength training and flexibility exercise are helpful to those with PPMS. According to Delgas and Stanager,

> It has been suggested that exercise (or physical activity) might have an impact on multiple sclerosis (MS) pathology and therefore slow down the disease process in MS patients. It was concluded that some evidence supports the possibility of a disease modifying potential or exercise (or physical activity) in MS patients, but future studies using better methodologies are needed to confirm this. (1)

For someone newly diagnosed with relapsing MS, when symptoms are just beginning, and there is little disability with walking or balance, it would be wise to embark on a course of strength training as described above. After all, there is ample evidence already cited of the benefits of exercise and strength training throughout life, even without a chronic disabling disease.

It is even more important to start strength training before disability begins to increase, i.e., when the EDSS shows a score of 2.0 to moderate 3.0. If the disability has progressed to 4.0, relatively severe disability to 6.0, assistance is required to walk, then it is even more essential to begin to prevent further disability—or perhaps even reverse disability, as Carol and I discovered. Of course, in collaboration with one's neurologist, it is essential to be on a disease-modifying drug and stay on it.

Gym Membership, Silver Sneakers

Gym membership is very desirable, as fitness centers offer a wide range of free weights, resistance machines and other amenities. For those 65 or older who are on Medicare Parts A and B or who have Social Security disability (SSI), then the Silver Sneakers program is available through many Medicare Advantage Programs with no or minimal premium. Silver Sneakers provides free membership for us at the Y and is available at some other fitness centers as well. The only premium we pay is for Medicare Part B which everyone pays anyway.

Working Out at Home

If gym membership is not an option, you can also work out at home at minimal cost. You can purchase at limited cost a basic set of dumbbells of 3, 5, 10, 12, 15 pounds or more, sometimes even used, Resistance tubes can be used to perform a variety of resistance exercises. A Pilates ring may also be used in flexibility training. Stability balls may be used if this can be done without risk of falling. If a caregiver can work out with you, that would be best.

Beyond that, a chair can be used to stand up, with or without using the arms of the chair to push up from. This helps strengthen the quads and iliopsoas. Using your arms to push up strengthens the triceps.

What You Can Do

Standing with the balls of your feet on a two-by-four board can be used to do calf raises. If it can be done safely, then having dumbbells in each hand or weights around the waist would be of benefit.

Full extension or modified push-ups may be done from a kneeling position if full extension push-ups are too difficult. Or modify the push-ups by pushing against a wall. Push-ups strengthen the pectoral and triceps muscles.

You can also do abdominal crunches or sit-ups while lying on the floor. Add Pilates movements, which strengthen the core. (*Details follow in the Addendum.*) Yoga mats make floor exercises more comfortable and prevent slipping.

Body-weight squats may be done routinely at home, strengthening the glutes and butt. For stability to prevent falling, these squats may be done from a chair.

Ari Meisel, who writes about squats in *The Daily Beast*, says:

> Squats are absolutely incredible. They build full-body strength as you use your core to stabilize and keep everything aligned. The glutes and hamstrings are very large muscles so buy [sic] utilizing them, you tend to burn a lot of fat.
>
> Squats invigorate your nervous system and help your stress response since the squat is a naturally defensive position. They can even help your digestion and the regularity of your bowel movements. This is essentially the Swiss Army knife of exercise. ... First off, if you can set a goal of trying to complete 100 squats each day you will see a noticeable change in your body in just a matter of weeks. (2)

The 100 squats do not have to be done in one set but may be spaced over the course of a day. The 100 number is a standard for someone without MS. Someone with MS may need to do fewer squats to avoid fatigue or risk falling. If you can do squats with stability and without risk of falling, you might also hold dumbbells in each hand to increase resistance and develop muscle mass.

An important benefit for the person with MS and his or her caregiver is being able to work out together. I do my own workouts between each of her sets, which allows Carol time to cool down. Joint workouts accrue benefits to our marriage. We consider our workouts "dates." There are a lot of couples at the Y who work out together, just as we do. One of those couples is a husband caregiver and wife who has MS.

Curiously, we see an upward spike in attendance at the Y after January 1st. Attendance levels off after a month or two; then we see the regulars. Motivation to change does not come through a New Year's Resolution.

Those with MS who do not have a caregiver will still need to work out regularly as described. It may be possible to find a friend to serve as a workout buddy or perhaps you'll meet someone at a gym who will become a workout partner. Just do it.

For someone with MS, the commitment to change comes from within, from the desire to live a healthier and happier life if the symptoms of MS can be slowed or reversed.

My motivation comes with the goal of living to the age of 104 and have everything working.

You know the saying, "Insanity is doing the same things over and over again and expecting different results." For those with MS who are experiencing increasing disability, it is all the more incumbent to begin the aggressive course of strength and flexibility training to change future outcomes for the better. Remember, you are responsible for how you respond to your illness.

Another saying I like is, "If what you are doing is not working, try something different." If what you are doing has not slowed or reversed your disabilities, try something different. Try strength training and flexibility training for six months and see what happens. You have nothing to lose except some disabilities. And don't let the negative people in your life deter you.

For Neurologists and Other Healthcare Professionals

I've heard some neurologists say they don't have time to tell their patients about exercise, and strength training in particular. I was surprised to hear a neurologist with a large practice in Knoxville tell us, "You have to be careful you don't become muscle-bound," I was taken off guard by that statement and said, "Women can't become muscle-bound." (The term "muscle-bound" connotes loss of flexibility.)

Heather has relapsing MS. She and her husband Chad are good friends. Heather has embarked on an aggressive training program with her trainer. He had worked with people who made the finals of *The Biggest Loser* on television. Heather's exercise regimen with him includes strength training. She is also following a gluten-free diet.

Heather and Chad have had remarkable results. She and her husband hiked a portion of the Appalachian Trail. She was told by her well-known neurologist and researcher at Vanderbilt, "Enjoy the gains while you can." This statement assumes the gains will not last.

I am greatly disturbed by these assertions by well-known and highly-regarded neurologists.

It is my assumption that most neurologists want the very best course of treatment for their patients. I believe they would like to slow the progression of disability and loss of function or even bring it to a halt if possible. Let me respond to their assertions.

♦ *Telling their patients they don't have time to discuss exercise and strength training.*

That can be done in 30 seconds and assigned to the office nurse under the authority of the doctor. When the doctor or office nurse tells patients they need to do strength training, this carries greater weight than someone who is not a physician. The office practice should have handouts about the benefits of exercise and strength training. They should also have a list of MS support groups and provide this book free, if they promise to read it.

Some patients will not take disease-modifying drugs. It is even more important to share information about the benefits of exercise with them, with the understanding that some will not act on the information. But some may. Remember, patients are responsible for their illness. Having said that, the patient can't take action unless the information is given and emphasized.

♦ *The assertion that, "You have to be careful you don't become muscle-bound," is an old expression but poorly defined and factually inaccurate.*

The concept of being "muscle-bound" is an old term used in some athletic circles, including major league baseball. It was believed for some time that weight training would lead to a loss of flexibility. This is simply not true. In modern athletic training, from high school through major league sports, including professional baseball, the NBA, NFL football, track and field, gymnastics and Olympic swimmers, training is done with a combination of resistance training and flexibility exercises. When Michael Phelps, Olympic gold medalist, is not in the pool, he is in the weight room.
The goal for someone with MS is not to become an elite athlete. It is to slow or reverse disabilities and improve one's quality of life.

- *To tell a patient who has shown improvement through diet and exercise, "Enjoy it while you can," assumes disability will progress regardless of what she does is a self-limiting and self-fulfilling prophecy.*

  A self-fulfilling prophecy becomes true because it is believed and acted on. This is more likely to happen if the person making the statement is a highly regarded expert in MS research. However, the statement is not backed by evidence-based research, particularly research in the area of strength and flexibility training. This should be researched in an observational study along the lines we have done.

  Carol and I attend many informational meetings sponsored by pharmaceutical companies over lunch or dinner. At one of these presentations, an MS nurse led a presentation about managing MS symptoms. She said that MS disability can't be reversed. At the conclusion of the meeting, I privately told her we had reversed Carol's disabilities with an aggressive course of strength training. There was no response. This was another example of an expert MS authority making a self-fulfilling prophecy to a room full of MS patients and caregivers. That statement by the MS nurse is often repeated, but in our experience, is not supported by evidence-based research or our personal successes.

- It was formerly believed that people with MS should not exercise. Later, that belief was dispelled after research proved otherwise. According to the National MS Society: "[We] are interested not only in potential drug treatment, but also lifestyle and alternative/complimentary treatments and we fund more research in this area than any other MS organization in the world. For example, studies funded by the Society played a pivotal role in reversing the mistaken belief that exercise was not a good idea for people with MS." (4)

I maintain that it is a mistaken belief that MS disabilities can't be reversed. Evidence-based research is needed.

Dr. Amy Myers, MD, who has an autoimmune disorder herself, states emphatically that n autoimmune disorder can be reversed. In her book, *The Autoimmune Solution*, she dispels many myths, the first myth being: Autoimmune disorders cannot be reversed.

We have often been told by well-intentioned people not to overdo it, meaning her strength training. Carol was even told that by her trainer. We didn't listen. We do listen to her body and the body doesn't lie. The body is a marvelous feedback system. In the normal course of her MS, fatigue levels vary greatly.

When her energy is low, we limit the intensity of the workout or the number of sets. But over the long haul, we continued to push higher weights as she made progress. Sometimes Carol hits a new high-water mark.

There is plenty of research on the benefits of exercise with MS patients. However, the studies I've found were limited to moderate exercise focused on the legs and core for as little as 30 minutes twice a week. According to Salynn Boyles,

> Researchers reported improvement in muscle strength and function and reductions in self-reported fatigue among eight patients involved in a two-month study evaluating resistance training. ... Training focused on the legs, lower back and abdomen for 30 minutes twice each week. At the end of eight weeks, the patients had significantly stronger muscles of the legs, were able to walk better and reported significantly less fatigue and disability." (5)

Another significant study discussed by Gretchen Reynolds in the *New York Times* found that,

... it is known that the first neuromuscular adaptations to
strength training are more neural than muscular. ... In fact,
in all research previously mentioned concerning strength
training in individuals with MS, no MS- related exacerba-
tions were reported and there were no reports of increased
MS-related symptoms. (6)

Dr. Samuel Hunter, MD, is an internationally known expert and
researcher in MS who practices an integrative approach to MS in
Franklin, TN. In private conversations with him, he has indicated to
us that strength training creates changes that are as much neural as
muscular.

The link between physical inactivity and changes in the brain
are also worth noting. In research published by in *The Science
Times*,

... exercise can remodel the brain by prompting the
creation of new brain cells and inducing other changes.
Now it appears that inactivity, too, can remodel the brain.
(7)

We believe that the positive changes in her vision, olfaction and
sexuality are due to the aggressive course in strength training and
flexibility training. Having said this, I have not found any studies on
aggressive resistance training and flexibility training neck to feet. I
would gladly lend my support as an advisor to any person or group
who wants to develop a rigorous study this subject.

There is Hope—Stop with the Excuses
If Carol can reverse her many MS disabilities as I have described,
then you may possibly slow or reverse your disabilities as well.
Slowing loss of function is a laudable goal. Just do it. You can have
excuses or you can slow or perhaps reverse disabilities, but you
can't have both. Maybe you promised yourself or someone else that

you would make a positive change in your life, but did not keep that promise. Stick to your commitment.

People often make excuses for not doing something that would be good for them. One favorite excuse is, "I don't have the time." Everyone has the same amount of time in a given week. There are many conflicting demands on our time. What is really happening is there is a failure to prioritize and make time for the things that are most important.

How much time is needed for aggressive strength training and flexibility exercises? Remember that even a moderate amount of exercise in a given week produces positive results.

To take our efforts to a higher level, we worked out Sunday through Wednesday about two hours a day with 20 minutes of rest between the fitness center and flexibility training. This was about 8 hours a week, plus or minus. Factor in a 30-minute round trip to the YMCA, and we spend a total of about ten hours a week doing our workouts. Now we have scaled back and work out Mondays and Tuesdays, followed by stretching and stretching only on Friday. Given our results, our commitment has been well worth it. Again, you can have excuses or have positive results—but you can't have both.

Another favored excuse is, "I don't think it will work." Or, "I don't think it will work for me." Really? And how did you arrive at that conclusion without committing to it for an extended period of time? We saw positive results in the first week and amazing restoration of function over two years.

For the most part, friends, relatives and caregivers are very supportive. On the other hand, the problem for people with MS is the negative reaction of some friends and relatives who may not be supportive of our program. They may belittle the efforts we have described that have the potential to slow or reverse disabilities. These people may be well-intentioned, but mistaken.

Remember, if you have MS, it is important to take charge of your life. No one else lives in your body or experiences MS as you do. You are the ultimate judge of your thoughts, feelings and behavior. Take responsibility for them; don't leave your life in anyone else's hands. If your caregiver can't or won't work out with you, then do it on your own. If you work out in a gym, find a workout partner or ask staff to assist you. Just do it.

Chapter 3—Endnotes

(1) Delgas, Ulrik, PhD; Stanager, Egon, MD, "Exercise and disease progression in multiple sclerosis: can exercise slow down the progression of multiple sclerosis?" Therapeutic Advances in Neurological Disorders, March 2012, 5(2), 81-95, 2012.

(2) Meisel, Ari, "Squats: The Absolutely Incredible Secret to Staying in Shape," *The Daily Beast*, 1/2/15

(3) Ibid.

(4) Rosenblat, Arney, Associate Vice President, Public Affairs, "Response to a Dear Colleague letter asking about Society dollars at work," National MS Society, September 1, 2010.

(5) Boyles, Salynn, "Pumping Iron Helps Strengthen MS Patients Study Shows Improvements in Muscle Strength, Fatigue, Disability," WebMD Health News, Jan. 19, 2005, ©2005, WebMD, Inc., All Rights Reserved

(6) Reynolds, Gretchen, "A Brain Boost From Exercise," *The New York Times*, April 16, 2013.

(7) Reynolds, Gretchen, "This Is Your Brain On the Couch," *The Science Times*, January 28, 2014, p. 4 .

CHAPTER 4

IN THE PROVIDENCE OF GOD

Some people believe that apparently random events happen and people meet by "chance," or "fate." As a theologian, I believe that these seemingly random events are in the providence of God. Two people may meet and never see each other again. Sometimes they only dance once. These meetings may be life-changing for both people. You may never know how the other person's life was changed. But your life and maybe the lives of other people around you become changed as well. This is in the providence of God. As Isaiah writes, with God speaking, says, "I am God, and there is none like me, declaring the end from the beginning." (Isaiah 46: 9b-10a RSV)

Carol and I met at a church singles group. She was divorced and I was separated from my estranged wife, intending to divorce. We met on my birthday, December 26th, and saw each other again on New Year's Eve at a party at her house. Our first date was January 2, 1988. She was looking for an intelligent man with a sense of humor she could date. She never expected to remarry. We fell madly in love. This was in the providence of God.

When two people become emotionally involved, they bring certain baggage to the relationship. Carol had an elderly mother, Kathryn, living with her and Stuart, her six-year-old son.

Carol and I eventually got married two years later on December 30, 1989. Kathryn and I got along reasonably well and Carol and I worked well together as team in raising Stuart. To this day, Stuart is grateful for all I did in raising him. All this was in the providence of God.

What would have happened to Carol if we had never met? As her MS and disabilities became progressively worse, it is likely she would have been in a wheelchair or living in assisted living or a nursing home.

We remain happily married. You know the story of how together we reversed her many disabilities and restored many lost functions. I thank God daily and I thank her for being the woman she is. We were meant for each other in the providence of God.

ADDENDUM

INSTRUCTIONS
FOR EXERCISES

INSTRUCTIONS FOR USING STRENGTH TRAINING & FLEXIBILITY EXERCISES

The following are instructions for using strength training and flexibility exercises to improve balance, strength, endurance, flexibility and overall quality of life for those who have MS. This is the regimen Carol and I have refined over the years.

Technique

◆ Drink ice water. Water will hydrate; ice water will cool through the core.

◆ Begin with lower weights and over time, keep increasing the weight as you gain greater strength. This will decrease the possibility of muscle soreness at the beginning. As weight increases, the number of reps will decrease quite naturally.

◆ Generally do 3 sets of each exercise. To begin with, do 15 reps per set and when you reach 20 reps, add another 5 pounds.

Reps may be reduced to 5 per set. If particularly fatigued, do fewer sets.

♦ During the exertion phase of the rep, push to full extension. Full extension will naturally decrease as you tire. Keep doing this until you can do no more.

♦ Breathe in through the nose during the relaxation phase and breathe out slowly over the lips during the exertion phase.

Exercise Regimen

Schedule workouts 4 to 6 times a week, alternating between arms and core, and legs and core. If you work out 6 times a week, take 2 days off for rest. At 4 times a week, take a day or 2 off to recuperate. If you do not work out that often, reduce the frequency to 3 times a week.

Core Exercises: The core is important in that the strength of the back and abdomen is critical; if you fall, you will have greater ability to get off the floor. In addition, your posture will improve, straightening from a bent-over position. You will also look better in clothes. With the **Back Extension** machine, do up to 20 reps or until failure. With the **Abdominal Crunch** machine, do up to 20 reps if possible. If you work out at home, do crunches or sit-ups lying on a mat and Pilates, which will be described later.

Legs: Work all leg systems, since the body functions synergistically.

♦ **Seated Leg Press** machine: Works buttocks and quads. Do 3 sets and maximum reps until failure and continue to increase weight to the maximum. (Use this formula unless otherwise noted.)

♦ **Seated Leg Curls**: Works hamstrings.

Back Extension

Abdominal Crunch

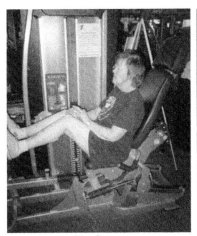

Leg Press

Leg Curls

- **Seated Adduction** machine: Works the inside of the thighs/ groin.

- **Seated Abduction** machine: Works the outer thigh/hips. Works the hips/thighs outward during exertion.

- **Standing Calf Raises** or seated **Leg Press**.

- **Thigh Lift:** With your back against the back pad, place your forearms on the arm pads. Lift your thighs to a horizontal position. This strengthens the iliopsoas.

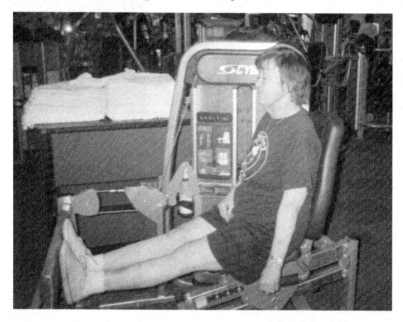

Calf Press

Addendum: Instructions for Exercises

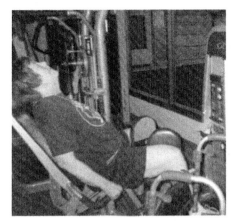

Adduction/Abduction Machine

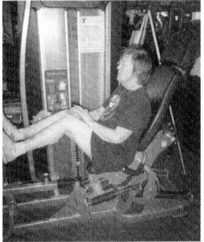

Leg Press

Leg Lifts

Leg Curls

Arms: Work all arm systems every other workout. Along with the core, the arms are necessary for balance and getting off the floor in the event of a fall. This will also aid in creating greater hand and finger strength.

- **Seated Press** machine: This works pectorals and triceps.

- **Seated Vertical Press** machine: Works deltoids and trapeziums. You may substitute dumbbells if doing this at home or if there is no Vertical Press machine.

- **Seated Concentration Curls:** With the dumbbell in one hand, place the elbow in the inner part of the thigh, then lift the dumbbell to the chin. Then alternate to the other hand. This exercise works the biceps.

- **Dead Lift:** It is important to have a spotter in the event you lose balance. With a barbell evenly spaced between your hands, lower the weight to the mid-shin or feet, then return to an upright position. Strengthens the lower back muscles.

Allow 15 to 20 minutes of rest between strength training exercises and stretching / Pilates.

Chest Press

Vertical Press

Triceps Extension

Seated Concentration Curl

Dead Lift

Balance, Stretching and Core Strengthening

- **Tai Chi Pose:** This is for balance. With one foot on the floor, lift one arm to a horizontal position and push the opposite leg forward. Hold for 30 seconds. Alternate to the alternate leg and arm. All exercises are for 30 seconds unless otherwise noted.

- **Hip Stretch:** Lying on the floor on a mat, with the right leg bent toward the chest and left leg flat on the floor, pull right leg to the left. Alternate with the left leg bent toward chest and right leg flat on the floor. Pull the left leg over to the right. Stretches the hip flexor.

- **Seated Hamstring Stretch:** In a seated position with legs spread apart, lean forward with arms reaching ahead as far as possible. Hold for 30 seconds. Then reach forward with arms over the left leg for 10 seconds. and then the right leg for 10 seconds.

- **Kegel Exercises:** While lying down, contract the anal and bladder sphincters for 30 contractions. This will improve bladder and bowel control.
  On days we don't exercise at the Y, Carol does these while riding in the car or at home. Kegels, coupled with medication, have been essential in her control of bladder and bowel function.

- **Foot/Ankle Strengthening:** With your workout partner, lie down on the mat while she or he puts isometric pressure against the feet, first pressing inward for 40 seconds, then pressing downward against the feet for 40 seconds, then outward for 40 seconds. Do three sets.

This may be expected to reduce or eliminate foot drop as it did with Carol.

Tai Chi Pose

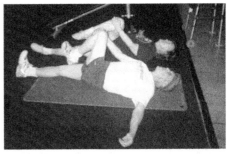

Hip Stretch

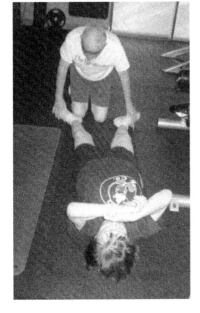

Ankle Strengthening

Hamstring Stretch

Pilates: Invented by German gymnast and bodybuilder Joseph Pilates, this is a physical fitness system that strengthens the core. Most exercises are done on a mat, the others standing.

- **Inner Thigh Press:** Lie on your back. Raise shins parallel to the floor in the tabletop position. Knees are bent and slightly apart. Place a yoga block or squishy ball between your knees. Inhale and then exhale as you squeeze your abdominals while squeezing the ball. Hold for 3 counts. Repeat 8 times. Do 2 sets of 8.

- **Heel Taps:** Lying on your back, lift one leg at a time into the tabletop position with shins parallel to the floor. Keeping the leg position of bent knee, tap the heel of the foot down onto the mat and then lift it back up again. Do not let the back arch. Do all you can to maintain your pelvic position and a stable spine. Repeat with the other leg in the tabletop position. Repeat 8 times for both legs.

- **Deltoid Lifts:** Sit up straight with your arms low and in front of you with wrists crossed. Make fists with your hands. Inhale to prepare, exhale to lift the elbows up to shoulder height while bending the elbows. Gently release to the starting position on an inhalation and begin again. Repeat 8 times.

- **Pilates Darts:** (Not shown) This is a back and abdominal strengthening exercise. Lie on your stomach with your arms at your sides and legs together. Lift your upper body/chest slightly off the mat. Keep your abdominal muscles pulled in. Your head is an extension of your spine. Your gaze will be down. Hold as long as possible. This strengthens the lower back muscles and will improve posture. It is also recommended for people with lower back pain.

- **Planks:** (Not shown) Lying on the mat on your abdomen, place your elbows on the mat directly perpendicular to your shoulders. Lift your abdomen off the mat for as long as you are able. Increase the length of time you can hold the position. This strengthens the lower back and abdominals. Posture should improve.

♦ **Wall Roll Down:** In a standing position with your heels about 6 inches from the wall and back against the wall, reach upward with your arms extended and reach down so that you are close as possible to touching your toes. Do 7 reps. Strengthens the back and abs.

Inner Thigh Press

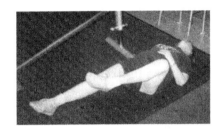

Heel Taps

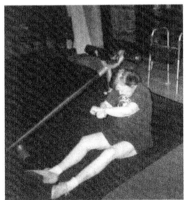

Deltoid Lift

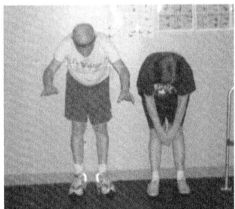

Wall Roll Down

Standing Stretching Exercises

Types of stretching:

♦ *Ballistic:* Bouncing through a stretch will not help lengthen muscles and may do harm. While popular in the 1970s and '80s, avoid.

♦ *Static:* Done at the end of exercise and strength training. Lengthens muscle fibers. Hold for 30 seconds and for the following stretching techniques.

♦ *Active:* Using opposing muscle groups to stretch muscles.

♦ *Passive:* Passive stretching takes muscles through their range of motion with the help of an external object, such as a towel, rope or help of a partner. If you cannot do these exercises by yourself, then have your caregiver or workout partner do the stretching for you.

♦ **Neck Stretch:** In a standing position, bring your right arm behind you. Tilt your head to the left as you pull gently with your left hand. Repeat on the other side.

Neck Stretch

- **Head Retraction:** Place your hand on back of head. Pinch your shoulder blades together as you push your head back. Stretches the upper back core muscles.

Triceps Stretch: Stand with your hand behind your neck and your elbow pointing upwards. Then use your other hand to push the elbow down, (or use a rope or towel), to pull your elbow down. If you can't do that, then have your workout partner stretch your triceps for you on the left side by holding your hand and pushing the elbow up with your left hand. Repeat with the other triceps.

Head Retraction

Triceps Stretch

- **Stork Position :** Also known as the Standing Quadriceps pull. Stand tall with abs engaged, feet together, with arms by sides. Bring left heel toward butt and grasp top of foot with right hand. Extend left arm out, (or place hand on a chair or rail to help balance). Bring the left heel of the foot as close to the butt as possible. Repeat on right side. If this is too difficult, have your workout partner lift your feet so your heels come as close as possible to touching your butt. This is what Carol and I do.

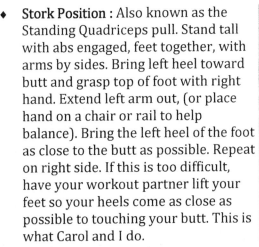

The Stork or Quadriceps Stretch

♦ **Calf Stretch:** Stand upright and lean against a wall or hand rail of steps. Place one foot as far from the wall as is comfortable and make sure your toes are facing forward and your heel is on the ground. Repeat with the opposite leg. Or, stand on a stair step with the ball of the foot on the edge and drop the heel to stretch the calf, then alternate to the other foot. Or, standing against a wall, place your hands on the wall, and put the ball of your right foot against the floor and lean forward into the wall. Stretches the calves.

Calf Stretch

Carol getting herself up from the floor. Stretching and Pilates

David and Carol Phillipy, the MS Warriors

God gives power to the faint, and to him who has no might he increases strength. Even youths shall faint and be weary, and young men shall fall exhausted; but they who wait for the Lord shall renew their strength, they shall mount up with wings like eagles, they shall run and not be weary, they shall walk and not faint.

Isaiah 40: 29-31 RSV.
This quote is printed on one of my t-shirts.

ABOUT THE AUTHOR

David Phillipy has spent most of his professional career as a prison chaplain, working in three different systems and five prisons. He continues to serve as volunteer chaplain at a maximum security institution. Much of his writing grows out of that experience.

His second marriage is to Carol Phillipy. Between them, they have four adult children, all boys.

David is driven by the belief that when he dies, his unwritten stories will also die. This is the spirit in which he has written this book, which is now the basis of a documentary film that he is producing, *The MS Warrior: A Love Story.*

Please visit www.themswarrior.com to view his trailer. Please contact the author to be placed on his mailing list as he and his team continue filming and seek distribution.

Author's Note

Whether or not one has MS, it is essential that couples and their children need to talk about in the event of death. These include having a will, a living trust when appropriate, and living will. Carol and I have talked about what we want to happen when we die. We agree it would be best that she should die before me because she is so dependent on me. We both want to have our remains cremated. The ashes can be kept in the columbarium at Trinity Presbyterian Church. If Carol predeceases me, then I would like to take her ashes to Maui, Hawaii, and sprinkle them in the ocean, or to Kauai, the Garden Island, in the ocean or in one of the scenic areas on land.

Please feel free to contact the author as follows:
Website: www.themswarrior.com
Email: dphillipy@comcast.net
Cell phones: (615) 554-5876 or (615) 373-5876

CPSIA information can be obtained
at www.ICGtesting.com
Printed in the USA
LVOW13s1050170417
531081LV00005B/755/P